Contents

Dreaming
and
Scheming

Smart planning starts with a vision—your dream of the way you want your house to live.

Go ahead: dream about what your house would be like if you added on. That big, roomy kitchen you've longed for—could it be within reach after all? Or how about that warm, sunny gathering space with a soaring ceiling and a cozy hearth, where the whole family congregates comfortably? Or maybe a serenely secluded master suite, complete with separate shower and tub alcoves?

Whatever notions you harbor about putting your house back in step with the way your family lives—or yearns to live—they needn't remain mere wishful thinking. Instead, use this book to bring your dreams to reality.

At some point you'll no doubt want to enlist a professional designer and/or builder to help convert your dreams into working drawings and boards-and-bricks reality, but the earliest—and the most important—stage of any remodeling project is the dreaming and scheming. And those activities should begin with you, not with outsiders. Only you know what your real priorities are regarding home and family, and what shortcomings are in your present house. Only you can decide whether you're ready to shoulder the financial burden to gain the space you're after and whether you can do part of the work yourself.

You don't need elaborately detailed sketches or drawings at this point—just your own enthusiasm and determination plus a penchant for clipping and pasting whenever you see images that echo your dream, and a habit of jotting down sudden inspirations before you forget them. Let your inner voices tell you what the new space should be. At this early stage of the project, you are the designer, and the more impact you have on the design, the closer it will come to making your dream come true.

Visions of an airy, generous-size family gathering space led to the creation of this open-beam hearthside sitting area, part of a second-story addition to a ranch home in California.

Start a Wish List

Before designers make a single drawing for a major building or remodeling project, they write up the project program—a paragraph-style outline of the main objectives and principal features that will give the design its shape, function, and look. The more carefully the program is spelled out, the more likely the project will meet the needs and expectations of the homeowners.

You can build in some extra insurance against disappointments or regrets by recording and organizing your ideas in a project wish list—a catalog of all the must-have, nice-to-have, and fun-to-have items that come to mind as you and your family envision what your house will be like after it has been expanded.

Ask key questions

To streamline your list-making sessions, ask yourself (and the rest of the family) a few key questions about needs, wants, goals, problems, and general suggestions. What are your home's major shortcomings? Take a

This bathroom addition includes a whirlpool tub—a must-have feature for many families when they build or remodel.

critical look at such aspects as living space, traffic patterns, outdated equipment or features, and lack of light or ventilation. In what ways have your family's needs changed since you moved in? Here you might note such things as crammed closets and cupboards, overworked bathrooms and laundry areas, lack of privacy for kids or parents, and inconvenient access to outdoor living areas. How will your needs change in the near future? Look ahead to your family's next life phase, when such things as becoming empty nesters or making room for live-in grandparents may suggest a different layer of priorities for expanding and updating your home.

Take some sensory snapshots

Not all the things you love about a house are purely functional; some appeal to your senses—the way sunlight warms a room, the cozy feeling you get when you curl up in front of a fireplace, the pleasure you get from seeing clutter disappear inside a bank of handsomely detailed built-ins. If images like the ones on these pages attract you as you thumb through home design magazines or visit real homes, they probably stick in your mind like snapshots in a mental photo album. The fact that they're so compelling makes them prime candidates to be included on your wish list as features or design details that you'll want your completed project to incorporate.

Pick a user-friendly format

Great ideas usually occur at random—sometimes when you least expect them—and a well-rounded wish list evolves over a period of months or years. You'll want to pick a format that lets you organize your list easily and then expand, revise, and edit it without having to rewrite or retype the whole list each time. An indexed card file is one option; to update the list, you simply add, delete, or reshuffle the cards. A better option is a text file on your computer.

Hearthside sitting areas are favorite features for rooms all around the house. This one replaces the original workspace at one end of an expanded kitchen.

Sample Wish List

Here is one suggested method of organizing the types of information you'll probably want to include on a project wish list. The project represented in this example is one of the most common types of remodelings: a one-story kitchen/family room addition.

Code:

■ Must have
■ Nice to have
□ Fun to have

New Family Room

■ Gas fireplace	brass trim	$2,000
■ Vaulted ceiling	exposed beams	
■ French doors to deck	two sets?	$800 each
■ Open to kitchen		
■ Big TV	60-inch HDTV	$1,500
■ Place for Christmas tree		
■ Open to stair landing		
■ Arches	over landing, above fireplace	
■ Electrical plugs in floor	for lamps, Christmas tree	
□ Leaded glass transoms	above French doors	
□ Remote-control shades	to avoid glare on TV	

New Kitchen

■ Island with cooktop	downdraft vent	
■ View of TV and fireplace		
■ Family eating area	bay window	
■ Built-in refrigerator	side-by-side	$1,200
■ Built-in microwave	near eating area	
■ Solid-surface counters	off-white	$10,000
■ Walk-in pantry		
■ Farmhouse sink	off-white	$400
■ Tile floors	stone look	$5 sq. ft.
■ Natural cherry cabinets	arched fronts	$50,000
■ Tile backsplashes		
□ Place for dog dish		

New Guest Room/Home Office

■ French doors to fam. rm.	one set	$800 each
■ Two workstations one PC	one desk	
■ Place for sofa bed or	Murphy bed	
■ Two closets	one clothes, one files	
■ View of garden		
■ Cove lighting	on dimmers	
□ Shelves for trophies	glass doors?	

Convert Old Kitchen to Mudroom/Laundry

■ Coats and boots cubbies	one for each of us	
■ Bench	storage underneath	
■ Folding space	white laminate	
■ Deep laundry sink	white	$200
■ Big hampers	roll out on casters	
■ Tile floor	stone look	$5 sq. ft.
□ Clothes chute from 2nd floor		

Exterior

■ Match roofline on house		
■ Match siding on house		
■ New deck, synthetic planks		
■ New service porch	square corner post	
■ Lattice screens	hide AC and meters	
■ Flagstone path to gate	or cobble pavers	
□ Dog door to fenced yard		

Begin by grouping your ideas according to the room or area where you think they'll be most likely to be used. Within each grouping, you may want to cluster similar-type items under subheads such as "Storage Built-in," "Surface Treatments," "Focal Points," or "Smart Splurges." Also leave space in each row of items to add descriptive notes and to plug in costs later (where applicable) when you've had time to track down that kind of information.

If you get an early start on your wish list and update it regularly, what you'll end up with is actually more than just a design program; it also will be the beginnings of a list of design and construction specifications (or "specs," as the pros call them) and a list of materials specs. Having this kind of data assembled and organized in advance is bound to save time and avoid misunderstandings later when you begin meeting with your designer and contractor.

Gather Ideas

A large part of the planning process for an addition project involves making decisions—about design features, special details, and products and materials you want to incorporate. Making these kinds of decisions is an even more complex task now than it was a decade or two ago, because the range of choices in any given category—such as countertop materials or window design—has exploded. Some homeowners let the designer or builder make most of these decisions for them—and the results aren't always what they hoped for. Others try to be more actively involved but wait too long to begin the selection process and end up having to make a lot of critical choices quickly and under pressure, with the designer or builder anxious to keep work progressing at the drafting table or the job site. You're more likely to make smart choices if you allow yourself time to look at a number of options and to sift through them in a more relaxed fashion. Therefore, the weeks or months leading up to your first meetings with your designer or contractor should be put to good use as a kind of crash course in home remodeling. In addition to the design ideas you have, see what other types of solutions designers have come up with recently for the type of project you're planning. Explore the latest products being offered for the types of spaces your project will include. Keep your eye peeled for clever little ideas or details that add that extra measure of style or livability you're looking for.

Snip, click, and surf

The range of choices may be multiplying exponentially, but so are the tools you can use for tracking them down and evaluating them. Even home design magazines have diversified considerably in recent years. Not only are there more new titles on the news-stands than ever before, there also are new varieties, including hybrid publications such as the magalog (a combination maga-zine-catalog), which offers valuable shopping information on products related to home building and remodeling. Also, tradi-tional-format magazines have beefed up their coverage of the marketplace by featur-ing product previews more frequently and by making their buying-guide sections more user-friendly. As you come across articles, items, or ads that target some aspect of your project, snip them out and start a collection. Any image that shows exactly what you have in mind will be a great help later when you sit down with your designer or builder.

Today's home design magazines provide a wealth of inspiration and expertise on a broad range of subjects— including style trends, floor-plan solutions, product buymanship, and do-it-yourself decorating.

When touring a show home, look for small details that could be adapted to your own project. These four photos, all taken in the same home, show examples of the kinds of details you're likely to see.

Another newly expanded source is televised home-design advice. Pioneered by the long-running weekly PBS show *This Old House*, home-design programs air almost continuously on various channels.

A few days of watching professional decorators and remodelers work their magic will familiarize you on the latest design trends. Most shows have websites to download additional information.

But the newest and most data-rich tool is the Internet. Here you can research your home's architectural heritage to make sure your addition will blend harmoniously.

If you want to tour model homes to get ideas on kitchen layouts, there are websites where you can use virtual-reality to "walk" through houses. If you're looking for a particular type of product, such as a vintage-style latch, the Web may help you find the only manufacturers in the country that still offer them.

Join the parade

Touring homes on the Web will open your eyes to design trends and product lines that you might not have known about otherwise, but there's no substitute for the real thing.

It's important that your idea-gathering tactics include live visits to model homes in your area. Usually, builders have a few furnished models on display year-round, and at least once a year the local chapter of the National Home Builders Association sponsors a Parade of Homes. Although these are new homes, not additions, they may incorporate design ideas and product innovations that could work for remodeling projects.

As you tour, jot down notes or pick up brochures on the features that pique your interest. Keep an eye out for exceptional design and construction; show-home tours are good places to discover qualified designers and contractors.

Start a scrapbook

Your idea-gathering is bound to yield an assortment of reference items—notes, clippings, sketches, business cards, paint chips, fabric samples, tile samples, and so on. Collecting them in a drawer or a cardboard box may keep them from getting mislaid, but accessing them is difficult when they're in a jumble. A more workable solution is to organize them into a scrapbook, preferably one with ring-bound pages so you can expand each section. A scrapbook is a good place to keep an updated copy of your wish

list. After you meet with a designer, your scrapbook also makes a handy place to file copies of sketches and preliminary drawings which you may want to refer to as you shop for finishes and furnishings.

In addition, a nicely compiled scrapbook will simplify the task a designer or contractor faces when it's time to help you develop plans and begin selecting products for your project. He or she will see style and color preferences, architectural details, and product features. The ideas or items you select might be ones that he or she hasn't considered before, so having an image or a manufacturer's address will make it easier to work those elements into the project.

Annual Parade of Homes tours feature several furnished show homes outfitted with the latest innovations in planning, products, and style concepts.

TIPS FOR ORGANIZING YOUR SCRAPBOOK

The outline below lets you arrange the items collected in your scrapbook. In addition to mounting them on ring-bound pages, add pockets on inside covers for quick access to key items.

1. Wish list—Keep an updated copy at the front of the scrapbook. Pencil in new information or reprioritize the list as you shop or meet with experts, then update your master file periodically.

2. Clippings, sketches, notes—Organize by room or area. Leave space for prices, product specs, design terms, etc. Label if they are design ideas, technical explanations, or tips on saving money or time.

3. Product samples—Categorize by room or area. Include real samples, brochures, snapshots, and other images. Add name and address of manufacturer, style name/number, color, price, etc.

4. Shopping sources—Organize by source or product category, including manufacturers, dealers, catalogs, classified ads, the Internet, and trade show venues. Leave room for key contact information.

5. People sources—Organize by source category, including designers, contractors, subcontractors, do-it-yourselfers, and lenders. For each, paste in a business card, brochure, or Web page print-out.

6. Drawings and documents—Keep copies of drawings or documents to refer to as you shop for products or attend meetings. (Keep originals filed elsewhere.) Arrange drawings starting with early sketches and ending with presentation drawings. To add items, cover the prints with tracing paper.

Talk to Experts

As you gather ideas and begin thinking more seriously about an addition, you'll probably have questions that are best answered by experts—either seasoned designers and builders, or knowledgeable product vendors. You don't neccessarily have to wait until you've hired a designer or builder of your own to tap into this kind of expertise. Some of it is available just for asking, or a nominal fee, and some is sitting just waiting for you in your local bookstores and library.

Face to face

Although one addition project may be all you ever tackle, some people do several—and serve as their own designer, contractor, or specialty trades worker—either to keep pace with major changes in their lives or to build equity without having to shoulder a huge mortgage. A few even do it full time, earning their living as professional remodelers. Chances are, several experienced remodelers in your area fit into one of these categories, but you're not likely to find them listed in the Yellow Pages.

Instead, you may hear about them via the local grapevine, by talking to neighbors who've remodeled recently or to dealers who sell building products, or by reading about them in the home section of the local paper. Often, seasoned remodelers—whether amateur or pro—are willing to share some of their expertise gratis or for a nominal consulting fee (or maybe just a nice lunch at the local steakhouse). They represent a gold mine of information regarding codes and regulations, techniques, dependable and not-so-dependable subcontractors, project-friendly lenders, and special sources for hard-to-find materials.

Another good source of information is the dealer or salesperson at the local wholesale and retail showrooms that specialize in a particular category of home-building products such as ceramic tile, windows and doors, flooring, or plumbing fixtures. Often the people behind these counters are former subcontractors who know the product category backward and forward because they used to earn a living installing that item at job sites. To cinch a sale, or to ensure customer satisfaction, they may be willing to share their field experience with amateurs who have questions.

Tips from a seasoned pro regarding matters such as which tile layouts require the least labor to install, which window frames hold their finish the longest, or which spas or hot tubs need extra framing for support underneath could potentially save you not only time, but also money and frustration.

Off the printed page

Even if no experts are available locally for face-to-face encounters, you can pick the brains of authors who've published books on the subjects of home building and remodeling. These are usually written by architects, designers, designer/builders, or enterprising do-it-yourselfers, all with a passion for creating and/or crafting one-of-kind personal shelters. Some authors focus more on style and design while others concentrate more on practical and technical matters (construction techniques, materials, etc.).

MAKE A PLAN

Talking to a salesperson at a retail or wholesale products showroom is a good way to pick up extra information about a given product category. Although wholesale companies normally sell only to contractors, their showrooms are usually open to the general public.

Either type of book can be helpful if you don't know much about designing and building houses, and either is likely to contain information that's applicable to additions. Although both types tend to deal solely with new construction, at the very least you're bound to pick up some building trades lingo that will come in handy during close encounters with designers, contractors, and job-site crew members once your own project gets under way. Full-retail cover prices for these publications run between $50 and $75—about what you'd pay a seasoned designer/builder for an hour's worth of private consultation.

Via plug and play

While you're at the library or bookstore, don't forget to check out the video department. Among the VHS tapes and DVD discs, you may find titles on home building, remodeling, and decorating. Some videos of this kind are excerpts or specific projects that aired within the last few seasons on HGTV or TV shows such as *Trading Spaces*, *This Old House*, or *Hometime*. Others are video "books" created by expert designers or designer/builders. One advantage of video format, of course, is that seeing the designs through the eye of the camera gives you more of a three-dimensional look than seeing them on the printed page. Also, it's easier to understand certain types of how-to demonstrations (such as how to install a light fixture) if you're able to see it done "live" on screen, step by step. If the kind of video reference material you're looking for isn't in stock, check for it at the order desk.

Other likely sources include discount building centers and the websites that are linked to the home-design TV shows. You can order the projects or segments you want either online or by calling the toll-free customer service numbers that are posted on the websites.

This restored Craftsman bungalow in Minneapolis is one of many rehab projects completed by husband/wife design team Terry and Camilla Hughes. Their experience and design savvy represent a rich resource for Twin Cities homeowners seeking to give their own homes a new lease on life.

Basic Design Strategies

During the early stages, sift down gradually to the scheme that will best achieve your goals.

The best solution for revamping this 1950s ranch involved adding up rather than out. This prompted a Craftsman-style makeover of the home's exterior, including stone piers, tapered columns, and rustic eave brackets.

A good chess player considers all the options before making a move. Likewise, a savvy remodeler considers all the basic design and construction options before zeroing in on a particular scheme. Although each remodeling project begins with a specific house and site, a specific budget, and a specific set of objectives (those of the family that lives there), there's likely to be more than one way to achieve those objectives. So it's important to keep your options—and your mind—open to alternatives that you may not have thought of or known about when you first started envisioning the end result. For example, "adding on" usually involves new rooms on the main floor, whereas the best way to gain the space you're after may be a lower-level or second-floor addition—or all three. Also, most new space for existing homes is constructed on-site from scratch (i.e., "stick-built"). However, your situation may lend itself to some type of prefabricated construction, which often costs less in the long run than stick-built and is much speedier.

Even if you already lean strongly toward one of the basic options discussed in this chapter, it's wise to weigh the advantages and disadvantages of all of them. Remodeling projects have a tendency to turn out somewhat different than envisioned, and sometimes the cause is an unexpected hurdle—such as a legal restriction or an irate, territorial neighbor. Staying flexible helps you deal with hurdles such as these, even when they require major shifts in design or construction strategy.

BEFORE

Construction Options

The type of construction option that will work best for your project depends on several factors. Some projects call for a great deal of custom design work, whereas others fit a more standardized concept. Some contractors specialize exclusively in stick-built, highly customized construction; others routinely work with a broad range of construction methods. Some sites pose special challenges that require a custom-designed, stick-built approach, whereas most others will accommodate any of several approaches. Which of the three basic options examined on these two pages looks like the right fit for your situation?

Stick-built

Additions are usually site-specific, and contractors who work on them tend to favor traditional, tried-and-true construction methods, so most projects of this type are built piece by piece on site. Other options are slowly gaining ground in the remodeling industry, but stick-built is a smart choice for projects that involve quite a bit of custom work to achieve a certain look or to get an exact match between existing and new. The chief advantage of stick-built construction is maximum design flexibility. Virtually anything you can dream up can be stick-built—assuming it fits your budget, of course.

If the addition you're envisioning will have unusual architectural features—such as an odd-shaped floor plan, an artfully sculptural exterior, or lots of rustic-cottage styling— or if matching your home's existing exterior calls for some painstaking, hand-built reproduction windows or trim details, stick-built is almost certainly your best choice. It's also the way to go if you're dealing with a tight site, one where the houses are built close together, the trees and shrubs are mature, and the yards are small. These conditions make it necessary to deliver materials to the construction area in small loads and to do all the heavy work with small-scale machines.

The main disadvantage of stick-built construction is that it's particularly labor-intensive. Building from scratch on site, piece by piece, means hiring expensive skilled labor to work on your project for several weeks or months. This not only drives up costs, it also causes a lengthy disruption of your household routine and generates considerable clutter and mess—debris, dust, litter, noise, traffic, parking problems, and so on. Also, lengthy construction means the project's financing plan will need to span the construction period as well as the years you'll actually use the new space.

Modular

If you're envisioning a fairly simple, straightforward addition and your site poses no special structural challenges, you may want to consider a speedier construction method. The speediest of all is modular construction. Most of the structure is built on the assembly line at a factory and then

This room addition is being framed the conventional way, with the floors, walls, and roof assembled on-site using dimension lumber and structural panels.

shipped to the site and erected in a matter of hours or days. Module sizes range from small bump-out bays to multiroom sections similar to large mobile homes. To achieve a custom look or to match the design of an existing structure, modules of various types can be assembled like giant building blocks, with room modules and dormered roofs stacked to form different levels.

Factory-based construction allows more efficient use of materials and more control over the quality of the work, and it eliminates many of the delays caused by weather. Also, since much of the work is done at the factory (the foundation and a certain amount of finish work still need to be done on-site), the usual mess and disruption associated with remodeling is minimized.

Kit-built

Like modular units, kits are manufactured on the assembly line under controlled, indoor conditions, then shipped to the site for erection by a local contractor (or do-it-yourself homeowner). And like modular units, kits are available in a wide range of types, from bump-out bays to multiroom structures. Kits have been used for addition projects for several decades. One common example is sunroom kits, which come in various shapes, sizes, and materials. Another is vacation homes, such as log cabins and A-frame cottages. As long ago as the early 1920s, kit homes were available from mail-order catalogs; today, semicustomized kit designs can also be ordered by mail either as additions or as new homes.

Kit-built additions are a particularly smart option if you're an experienced do-it-yourselfer and can do some of the erection work yourself. Also, kits make good sense if your design is fairly simple but your site is too problematic for delivery and erection of whole modules. Kit manufacturers tend to offer more design flexibility than those who

produce modular units, because varied component combinations lend themselves more readily to packaging and shipping requirements. However, like modulars, kit-built additions require site-built foundations. They also require more on-site construction labor and generate more construction debris and household disruption (though not as much as stick-builts do).

The one-story addition to this two-story Colonial arrived at the site in four modules—each one small enough to be shipped on a flatbed truck. The entire shell was assembled with a crane in less than two days.

Bumping Out

The curved bump-out bay in this remodeled kitchen houses a spacious family dining area, freeing up floor space in the rest of the kitchen for a generous-size island work center and twin banks of built-ins. The bump-out's tall casement windows capture views of the front garden while its skylight snatches extra sunshine.

One of the simplest types of additions is the bump-out. Technically, a bump-out involves pushing out an exterior wall no more than three or four feet—the maximum distance that wood floor joists can be cantilevered without adding foundation support. Loosely defined, however, a bump-out is any addition in which an exterior wall has been moved out several feet to make a room larger. Some bump-outs span the length of an entire exterior wall, adding space to two or more rooms at once.

Multiple benefits

Bumping out is an easy way to gain some of the same kinds of benefits that full-scale room additions offer. Besides providing extra floor space, bump-outs can open up a room to extra daylight, a more expansive view, and better cross ventilation. One

common type of bump-out, the sunspace bay, accomplishes all three because it usually includes wraparound windows, all or some of which are operable. Bump-outs can create extra floor space indirectly, by housing built-in storage units (such as a china closet or media wall) that otherwise would eat up existing floor space in a room. They also can provide extra elbowroom by incorporating bonus work space, such as a kitchen cabinet or a bath vanity. Another major benefit of bump-outs is cost; because they normally don't require foundations or extensive roof framing, they're much cheaper to build than a full-size room addition. Furthermore, their simpler, smaller form makes them easy for seasoned do-it-yourselfers to

build, and therefore offers even more opportunities for cutting costs. And if no foundation is needed, bump-outs offer a way to steal a few extra square feet of space where setback restrictions rule out a full-size addition (setbacks normally apply only to that portion of the house that rests on a permanent foundation).

Not all the benefits of bump-outs are purely practical. Depending on how they're designed and where they're placed, bump-outs can provide aesthetic benefits, too. Bumping out part of a long, blank exterior wall can add architectural interest to an otherwise drab or unfriendly facade. They also can be used to lend emphasis (and extra protection from the elements) to an entry area.

MAKE A PLAN

If your plans include a bump-out that will affect the exterior of your home, don't forget to budget money for landscaping. Your site will suffer damage as workers and heavy equipment come and go, so you will want to plant trees, grass, and flowers upon the project's completion.

Suite Stretch

Despite its sunny hillside site, the master bedroom in this 1960s-era California ranch had been dark and dingy and lacked access to the poolside living area directly outside. Although the exterior wall could be bumped out only 3½ feet, that's all it took to give it the breathing space it needed. The extra square footage adds just enough room indoors for a suite-style sitting area near the bed, and the new exterior wall features two sets of glass doors that open the room to the outdoor living area.

To maximize floor space, the glass doors slide rather than swing. A tall casement window on one side of the bump-out provides cross ventilation plus additional glimpses of the rear garden from the bed and the sitting area. Easy access to a trellised deck and hot tub through the glass doors amplifies the room's spacious, private-suite feel.

Thoughtful design makes the bump-out look as though it had always been there. Its roof pitch, eaves, and siding match those of the existing structure, and a new deck merges it with the pool and the hillside site.

Adding Headroom

A flat-roof dormer on the back of this Tudor cottage created space at the head of the stairs for a sunny sitting nook outside the master bedroom.

Another relatively simple, low-cost way to boost square footage is to convert unfinished or underused space overhead. If your house or garage has an attic that's lying idle because the roof pitch is too low and there aren't enough openings to provide adequate light and ventilation, reworking your roofscape may be a much more affordable strategy than adding on at ground level.

Adding dormers and skylights

In attics that already provide headroom under the highest part of the roof, dormers or skylights may be all that are needed in order to make most of the floor space livable and eliminate the dreary, tunnellike effect that's often characteristic of under-eaves areas. Even a single one-window dormer or narrow skylight can make a big difference in a modest-size room, by adding valuable headroom, balancing the daylight, and providing cross ventilation. Twin dormers (on the same slope or on opposite slopes) or a double-window dormer multiplies the benefits considerably, making an under-eaves room feel almost like a full-height room.

For maximum space gain, you may want to consider dormers that run almost the full length of the roof. (This approach usually requires reworking your roof's structural framing, a job best handled by an experienced contractor or structural engineer.) Roof windows, a relatively new option, combine the advantages of a skylight and a dormer. They mount on a sloped roof like a skylight but can be swung or pivoted open like a dormer window, and come equipped with screens and shades. One version unfolds outward to form a mini balcony.

Like bump-outs, dormers and skylights are projects that a seasoned do-it-yourselfer could tackle, so they offer additional potential for cost savings. Of the two, a skylight is probably the simplest and quickest option. But both require carpentry skills and involve working on high ladders and roof slopes, so you may want to have a contractor do the installation.

Raising the roof

If your attic is minimal or your roof is pitched quite low, you may want to consider extending the pitch on one side or the other in order to gain adequate headroom. In a sense, what this amounts to is converting part of the roof into one large dormer, but it also involves extending one or both of the gable walls of the house plus a side wall, so the result is really more than just a dormer. Because a whole section of roof is raised, the enlarged space gains full-height walls on at least three sides, allowing ample room for partitions and windows. Some roof extensions angle upward to allow for clerestories or light scooping windows, a great way to give attic rooms extra daylighting, and dramatic vertical stretch.

The low-pitched ceiling in this attic bathroom is barely noticeable—thanks to an operable skylight that delivers fresh air, soaring views of the treetops, and extra inches of precious headroom.

Grand Opening

The attic above this 50-year-old ranch in Maine was larger than average and had considerably more headroom than that of most ranch homes of this vintage, but only a small portion at one end was livable. The rest was airless, dark, and unfinished. The only access was a narrow, steep, ship's-ladder staircase. To open up the space and make it more usable, a series of evenly spaced dormers were punched through the roof, banishing the gloom and offsetting the tunnellike effect of the sloping walls.

More livability up and down

The newly claimed square footage houses a guest room and a home office, freeing up family bedrooms on the main floor that had to do double duty before. At the other end of the main floor, part of an oversize living/dining room was partitioned to create a foyer and stair hall. This allowed room to replace the ship's ladder with a gracious, traditional-style staircase.

Putting attic space to work can have a domino affect on your home's livability too. As you develop a plan for using newly gained square footage overhead, think also about how you might shuffle or rework existing spaces downstairs. Creating more room up for children or guests could make way on the main level for the kind of master suite you've always dreamed of having. Or it might allow you to reconfigure your family spaces by converting one of the main-floor bedrooms into a book-lined getaway space, recycling the formal living room into a dining room big enough to handle the whole clan at holiday gatherings, and upgrading the family room to great-room status.

Adding dormers helped give this ranch a new look outside plus extra stretch inside. Their classic gable fronts repeat the roof pitch of the original structure. New windows, siding, and porch columns complement the dormers' classic simplicity.

BEFORE

White walls and minimal window treatments let the dormers capture maximum light and bounce it into the attic spaces. Storage built-ins hug the kneewalls in each dormer.

Adding a Room

Adding a full-size room on the main floor is generally more costly than bumping out or converting attic areas but it offers certain distinct advantages. Boosting main-floor square footage is usually the chief advantage, of course, and extra roominess in that part of the house is especially important because that's where your family spends most of their time together. A new family room, a spacious eating area, a master suite, or a den/home office is bound to make your home more livable and increase its value, particularly if it lacks these spaces now.

When envisioning a room addition, it's important to factor in other, less obvious advantages. For instance, a new room opens up your house in a new direction, one with views your existing rooms don't have. Also, the new room will have at least two or three full-height exterior walls, which presents a unique opportunity to flood the space with daylight. You may even want to add a large archway or cutouts in the old exterior wall to allow some of that light to brighten existing spaces. Sunspaces, one of the most popular types of single-room additions, sometimes take this notion a step further by incorporating skylights or glass panels in the roof design, creating a room that feels almost like an outdoor space.

Design challenges

One-room additions pose certain design challenges that need to be addressed before you firm up a set of plans. First, it's easy to miscalculate the amount of floor space you'll actually need and end up with a room that's either inconveniently cramped or uncomfortably barn-like. For best results, sketch a furniture arrangement to scale on graph paper, then add traffic lanes where you think you'll need them. Be sure to allow for door swings (including those on cabinets or appliances), space to push back chairs from desks or tables, and special spots for holiday-related displays or activities. Draw

COMMON TYPES OF FOUNDATIONS

Post and pier
- Minimal excavation needed
- Adapts easily to irregular terrain
- Low cost—uses minimal materials, simple carpentry skills

Slab-on-grade beam
- Minimal or no excavation needed
- Works best for flat, stable terrain
- Moderate cost—involves one construction trade rather than several
- Poses special challenges for utility runs

Concrete block on poured footing
- Substantial excavation needed
- Adapts to somewhat irregular terrain
- Moderate cost—involves skilled labor and heavy machinery
- Creates crawl space or basement for installing utility runs

Reinforced concrete with integral footing
- Substantial excavation needed
- Adapts well to irregular terrain
- High cost—involves skilled labor and heavy machinery
- Creates crawl space or basement for installing utility runs

Pressure-treated wood on crushed-rock footing
- Substantial excavation needed
- Adapts to somewhat irregular terrain
- Moderate cost—involves skilled labor and heavy machinery
- Creates crawl space or basement for installing utility runs

MAKE A PLAN

Windows can be one of the most important considerations in the design of your addition. A well-designed window plan can make your home appear larger and more spacious. And by purchasing good quality windows, you will immediately increase the value of your home.

walls around what you've sketched and then calculate the square footage they enclose. Second, make sure that the new space will be properly heated and cooled. Maintaining comfortable temperatures is technically more difficult in a room with three exterior walls than in a room with only one or two, especially if you live in a four-season climate

and want lots of window areas in the new space. If you're adding a modest-size room (10×12), your current heating, ventilating, and air-conditioning (HVAC) system can probably handle the extra load; for larger spaces, consider installing extra ducts, a heat-circulating fireplace, or an additional small-size HVAC unit.

This sunroom points up a chief advantage of single-room additions: being able to scoop in light and views from three sides. The Palladian-style window in the end wall frames a scenic vista. French doors on one side open to a new deck.

27

Trading Spaces

Smart design merges new with old. Siding and windows on the addition match those on the house, and broad steps and a stacked-stone retaining wall form a graceful transition between the addition and the rear terrace.

Sometimes, the spot where you need extra living space is already taken—by a garage, carport, porch, or storage shed. Playing a little floor-plan hopscotch may be the solution to this dilemma.

The family-room addition shown on these pages replaced a double garage that had monopolized a choice bit of real estate adjacent to the kitchen and the rear terrace. A new garage was constructed at the other end of the house, facing the street. In this example, most of the garage was recycled because it was sturdy and its footprint was the right shape for the new room. Some

existing structures are either too small or too flimsily constructed for reuse, but removal is usually a fairly simple matter—and well worth the extra space gained.

Thoughtful design makes this family room more than just bonus square footage. The original garage doors were replaced with a stacked-stone fireplace and twin banks of built-in storage units. Deep windows along one sidewall overlook the rear terrace, and the ceiling follows the roof pitch on both sides, adding architectural drama and an extra measure of spaciousness.

Finishes and detailing in the new family room echo the home's classic 1940s ranch character. Narrow-strip oak flooring matches that in the older part of the house, and simple Doric columns frame the wide archway that was cut into the old exterior wall. Raised-panel doors on the built-ins hide the TV.

A Craftsman-style canopy and a wide stoop form a space-saving "porch" outside the French doors. Angling the doors helped keep most of the patio intact.

Just Big Enough

The old adage "small is beautiful" rings especially true in this family room addition in Seattle. Measuring barely 14×18 feet, it fits snugly into a tight patch of ground between house, garage, and patio. The owners yearned for an informal gathering spot in their 1927 bungalow. Realizing the limits imposed by the tight site, they focused on a modest set of objectives: a hearthside sitting area just big enough for two comfy chairs, a dining nook that seats four, and easy access to the outdoors. The new room fulfills all three objectives beautifully, without gobbling up precious patio space or upstaging the home's simple bungalow charms.

A few subtle design tricks make the addition look and live much larger than its actual dimensions. Transom-top French doors and a pair of double-hung windows turn the dining nook into a glass-walled bay, *below*, making the patio seem like an integral part of the room. The old end wall in the kitchen was removed, allowing the two spaces to work as one—and to feel twice as big. Most of the furniture was built in, leaving space to flow freely around the two easy chairs and the table grouping.

The kitchen was updated as part of the remodeling, and opened to the new room. A snack bar replaced the original exterior wall.

To maximize floor space, the fireplace bumps out several inches under the roof overhang, and all of the storage units are built in. Simple, small-scale furnishings help make the room feel even larger.

Adding an Open-Air Extension

Although technically not considered rooms, most outdoor spaces added to a house are room-size or larger and have the same basic elements—and some of the same features and amenities—as a regular room addition. All require a proper foundation and solid floor construction, and many also involve some type of cover plus a sturdy structure to support it. In short, open-air extensions have everything that indoor rooms have except solid exterior walls. They therefore require a similar amount of planning, labor, and expense in order to do a good job of boosting your home's livability and value.

Wide range of options

The simplest open-air "room" is a single-level deck or terrace with no cover. However, it's also the most limited in terms of livability because it provides the least protection from the elements. Adding a cover, such as a trellis or awning, boosts livability considerably but also introduces extra structural and aesthetic considerations. A full-fledged open porch, complete with posts, railings, and pitched roof, offers a sense of enclosure and protection similar to an indoor room. Adding screen panels heightens this sense of subtle enclosure—and allows you to enjoy the space without having to arm yourself with flyswatters and bug spray.

Climate-savvy design

When planning an open-air extension, taking climatic conditions into account seems obvious, yet it's easy to get carried away by the romance of a porch or deck design and end up with a structure that's uncomfortable or uninviting much of the time and, therefore, a poor investment. For instance, if you live in a temperate climate where it's too hot to sit for long periods of time in full sun yet too chilly to sit in deep shade, neither an open deck nor a solid-roof porch is likely to be a sensible option. Instead, you probably should aim for a structure that provides dappled or tempered shade, such as a trellis or some type of translucent canopy. If you live in a cool climate or a heavily shaded neighborhood and are planning to add a porch, you may want to include skylights or a trellised section in the roof design to avoid creating a space that feels chilly or oppressively dark all the time. And if your climate is quite changeable from day to day or season to season, consider a "hybrid" design—part open deck, part trellised deck, and part covered porch.

Other key design considerations

Other factors to keep in mind as you picture the perfect open-air addition for your home are function and maintenance. Will you need room to seat several people, or just one or two? Will you want an area for dining as well as for seating? Will you need space in the addition to store furniture and accessories when they're not in use? One mistake often made in porch and deck design is making the space too narrow for a comfortable seating arrangement. (A minimum depth for porch seating plus a traffic lane in front of the people who are seated is approximately seven feet.) Another common mistake is including details or materials that require labor-intensive maintenance. Gingerbread, fretwork, lattice, spindles, and other trimmings that give open-air spaces great charm can also be big headaches unless you choose the right materials and finishes. Fortunately, painted wood is no longer the only option for decorative elements like these; you can instead have them in stained or naturally weathered wood (paint is an extremely high-maintenance finish for exterior surfaces) or in molded plastic versions that require no painting or staining whatsoever.

MAKE A PLAN

Sunrooms and porches are among the most popular additions because they extend a home's living area. The design of your sunroom or porch depends on your needs and your budget. If you are looking for a cozy getaway, then a small porch attached to the back of your house may suit your needs. If your goal is to provide an area to entertain guests, then your plans should include a larger space close to the kitchen.

The pleasing proportions of this porch addition imbue the front of the house with a whole new personality. Stout columns and a sheltering roof extend a warm welcome

Come Rain or Shine

Stone-clad piers, stained shingle siding, redwood beams, and natural-finish cedar flooring and ceiling keep maintenance chores to a minimum on this porch/deck addition.

The cool, changeable climate of the Pacific Northwest helped shape the design of this 24×36-foot outdoor room in Washington state. Added to one side of a 1919 Craftsman-style lake cottage, the new space directly adjoins the kitchen and dining area. The kitchen door opens to the portion of the room that's designed as a covered porch. Here, deep eaves and a gently pitched roof

provide shelter from frequent drizzles and downpours. The south portion of the "room" is a spacious sundeck that overlooks the lake. Exposed beams and an open gable in the roof give the porch an airy feel even on overcast days, and pale wood decking throughout softly bounces light into the back corners. Built-in benches provide extra seating for large gatherings.

Open-Air **Hospitality**

Warm, humid summers and a heavily shaded backyard set the scene for this pergola-style open-air "room." Part of a kitchen/family room wing added recently to a one-story home in Maryland, it combines porch-style elements with a classically formal raised terrace. Thanks to a thick canopy of foliage, the terrace gets direct sun only a small portion of the day, so there was no need for a solid roof—just gentle tempering of the sun's rays with trellises. Classic white columns, pilasters, and railing create a roomlike sense of enclosure while allowing light to flood the kitchen through a set of French doors. Brick piers supporting the columns tie the terrace to the house and extend as extra seating.

Generous proportions in this open-air space provide ample room for lounging, dining, and cross traffic between house and lawn. The crisp white columns and beams of the pergolas help tie the house to the yard and soften the facade's red brick walls.

Backyard Breeze-Catcher

The use of natural-finish cedar for the geometric fretwork and skirting of this porch addition eliminated the need for periodic scraping and repainting. Inside, a 13-foot-high ceiling and a paddle fan help keep the space cool on hot, muggy days.

Inconvenient access to the backyard and the need for a cool, breezy retreat on hot summer days prompted the owners of this two-story home in suburban Chicago to add on a screened porch. Although the yard is rimmed with tall trees, the back side of the house basks in direct sun most of the day, so the new porch was given a low-slung hip roof with deep overhangs on three sides. Double doors in the front wall of the porch open to stairs that lead down to the rear terrace and yard on one side and the driveway on the other. Natural cedar paneling on the inside and cedar trim on the outside give the porch a warm, rustic feel, tying it to its woodsy backyard setting.

BEFORE

Hillside Haven

Perched in the middle of a steeply sloping yard with tree-shaded views of the neighborhood on three sides, this house offered no place to enjoy the expansive vistas except from indoors. And to reach the front door, visitors had to climb a long set of steps that marched straight up the hill from the street. A large wraparound porch conquered both these problems beautifully—and gave the front of the house a friendly new face.

Measuring more than 8 feet deep, the front portion of the porch offers ample space at one end for a cozy grouping of lounge chairs, occasional seating, and small tables, plus plenty of open floor space for kids to play outdoors without rolling downhill. Around the corner, the porch becomes an open-air foyer outside the front door. The front steps now jog around one side of the porch and curve up the hill toward the entry at a gentler angle, creating pleasant spots to pause and enjoy the view on the way up.

Comfy chairs on this new front porch invite neighbors to linger for a chat. Simple details extend a friendly welcome: curved brackets and lattice skirting.

BEFORE

Adding Several Rooms

Bumping out or adding a new room can give your house an extra dimension of livability and even help create a fresh new look inside and out, but adding several rooms can trigger a whole different magnitude of change. For instance, there are limits to the number of problems you can solve with a one-room project, whereas with a multiroom strategy you may be able to address every single one of your home's current drawbacks or shortcomings, especially if your game plan includes revamping some of the existing spaces.

A new family room gives a house extra stretch; a new family room/kitchen wing that includes a full-size laundry area, a new mudroom, a first-floor powder room, and a home office makes a house function as if it's a different house altogether. Some multiroom projects do much more than simply overcome shortcomings; they shift the whole focus of the house to a new area or type of space and change it's personality inside and out. This is particularly likely if you're expanding and revamping the active areas of the house—main-floor spaces that set the tone of the household and provide a backdrop for various types of family gatherings. It's not uncommon for a multiroom addition to dramatically alter a home's main axis, shifting everyday activities from the front rooms to the new spaces out back, and maybe even relocating the formal entrance to put it more in synch with the home's restructured traffic pattern—and the family's new lifestyle.

Think out of the box

To make sure you tap this potential, think as broadly as possible in the early stages of planning. A multiroom addition needn't be just a one-level, boxes-within-a-box appendage; it can take any of several basic configurations, depending on the limitations of your budget and your building site. Should you build entirely on one level, or would the new addition function more efficiently—and fit in more seamlessly—if it contained two or three levels? Should it attach to one wall of your existing house, or wrap around the corner? Should it be a direct extension of your house, or should it be more like a freestanding structure connected to the house by a transition space (such as an informal entry or gallery)? Should it be a single unit attached to one part of the house, or multiple units attached at different spots in order to address each problem strategically?

As you weigh the practical advantages of these various alternatives, consider also how each of these basic options might deliver some interesting fringe benefits—special new features or attributes that your house currently lacks. For instance, multiroom additions offer great opportunities to generate architectural drama, particularly if the rooms are on different levels or if they include one large space that opens into several smaller ones. Soaring ceilings, cantilevered balconies, clerestory windows, and cascading staircases can give your house a whole new focus—and a new dimension of visual excitement. So can eye-catching vistas, both interior and exterior. Laying out rooms or levels and locating openings in ways that allow far-flung views (in the building profession these are called "through views"), unexpected glimpses, or picture-frame scenes can give otherwise plain spaces a lot of visual punch for relatively little money. They also can make modest-size spaces seem larger.

Don't overlook the potential of leftover square footage—small scraps and slices of space between rooms that usually get ignored or covered up in homes that are built from stock plans. Examples include stair landings, dead space under eaves and staircases, and odd-shaped spaces created by angled walls. Depending on their size, shape, and location, such leftovers can be put to work as storage cubbies, turned into eye-catching display areas, or outfitted as cozy getaway nooks, thus adding character and visual charm that most standard-plan homes lack.

Balancing act

One other factor to keep in mind as you ponder the various basic configurations that your addition might take is that the two volumes of space you'll be working with, your existing house and the new addition, need to be visually and functionally bal-anced once the project is finished. The amount of space in a multiroom addition often equals or exceeds that of the existing structure, and this can pose a number of tricky design challenges. Some are aesthetic, some have to do with technical or legal issues, and some involve the day-to-day liv-ability of the new and existing spaces in the house (see tip box, *below*, for examples). If your house and lot are fairly sizable and your addition is small by comparison, the balancing process will be an easy one. But if your lot is small and your house and addition are similar in size, you'll need to rely on good design to avoid creating "the addition that ate the house." The challenge will be to make them work together properly and to make it look as though they belong together. In fact, what you should aim for, even if you're unable to achieve it in the fullest sense, is a design solution that makes the addition look as though it was "always meant to be"—a solution that makes your house seem more complete now than it ever had been.

SOLVE DESIGN HURDLES ON MULTIROOM ADDITIONS

Maintain the buildable area ratio—Local codes may limit how much of your lot can be covered by structures (house plus outbuildings). A large addition may exceed the allowable ratio of structure to open space.

Coordinate the proportions of new versus existing volumes—Size, shape, and placement of an addition should be such that it doesn't overwhelm or upstage the original structure.

Avoid awkward siting—If poorly sited, large additions or additions on tight sites can create long, alleylike spaces next to garages, fences, or neighboring houses. Such spaces are difficult to landscape and put to use. Offsetting some of the new rooms or breaking up long, flat exterior walls with jogs, bays, or bump-outs are some of the ways to overcome this problem.

Maintain an attractive roofscape—If the ridgelines of the addition protrude above those of the original structure (a common situation where the addition is wider or deeper than the original footprint), they may create an unsightly hump that disrupts the continuity of the original roofscape. Also, if the roof planes on the addition are more complicated and at a different pitch than those on the existing house, the results may look like two structures "shoved together."

Three-in-One Stretch

The one real drawback to this suburban New York home was lack of space for informal living. The solution was therefore relatively simple: a 16×22-foot addition to the rear. Although the addition is actually three separate spaces—a family room, a new kitchen, and a new breakfast nook—they all fit together as a unit, neatly filling in the open space between the old kitchen and a detached garage. The garage is now part of the house, and the old kitchen became a formal dining room.

Even though the floor plan for the new spaces is quite simple and straightforward, it gives the house a whole new dimension of roominess and architectural drama. There are no interior partitions; the kitchen's base cabinets are the only walls, so the three spaces function as one main room, with uninterrupted interior vistas plus a handsome focal point—a tall storage wall at one end that houses the TV. Big windows and French doors merge the new room with a patio out back and with the formal living room up front.

The addition connects the house to the garage, forming a single L-shape structure. A new patio and the bump-out that houses the new breakfast nook nestle in the crook of the L.

If your addition includes a new or remodeled kitchen, take into consideration kids who live at home. Kids can work more comfortably in the kitchen if you design a kid area that includes a lower-than-standard counter, preferably between 28" and 34", and a second sink. You may also want to consider locating the microwave at a height convenient for easy access.

The new kitchen is open to the family room on one side and to the dining room (the old kitchen) on the other. Minimal upper cabinets let space—and conversation—flow freely through all three areas.

A vaulted, exposed-truss ceiling and a custom-built storage wall give the simple rectangular addition a bit of architectural flair. Locating the TV in the storage wall makes it visible from the kitchen work area and the dining room.

Targeted Problem-Solvers

Like the modest-size tract home on the previous two pages, this one in Massachusetts suffered growing pains. But in this case the problem was more complex; it called for several small additions rather than one large one.

On the street side of the house, the front entry needed to be moved and reconfigured as an entry bump-out to provide a buffer between the front door and the living room. Also, a jog on one of the front corners needed to be filled in to house a sunroom-style family work space, which would take some pressure off the dining room and kitchen. At the opposite corner, a master suite needed to be added so that the existing first-floor bedrooms could be recycled as a home office and a dressing area.

Although it cost extra to build each of these small additions as a separate unit, the owners were able to do them in stages as finances permitted. Also it was still cheaper to remodel than to build a new house from scratch that would have all the features they needed. Adding on gave them some "wiggle room" in their budget for upgrading some of the existing spaces and adding custom touches here and there—netting character and livability that's lacking in many new homes.

The old front door, which bisected the front wall of the living room, was relocated at one end in a new bump-out. Now there's room for a vestibule and a coat closet inside, plus a covered porch outside.

Although it has the feel of a glassed-in porch, the sunroom is outfitted as a work space for family crafts, with storage cabinets lining the walls under the windows, and a big work table in the middle.

A wing addition out back houses the master suite, which overlooks a new patio that adjoins the dining room and kitchen. Window muntins, siding, and trim in the new wing match those of the original structure.

43

Seeing Double

One thing this 80-year-old Dutch Colonial home had in abundance was character, but its rustic shingle-style details disguised some serious shortcomings—no informal living space downstairs and a cramped bedroom layout upstairs. A two-story addition seemed to be the best remedy, and there was ample room for expansion along one side, but what could be done to make the addition look like it belonged? The answer was to repeat the original structure's gambrel rooflines and to extend the entry porch as a rambling, gallery-style veranda.

Inside, the addition houses a family room, breakfast nook, powder room, and expanded kitchen on the main floor, and a luxuriously roomy master suite on the second floor. A wide arch merges the back half of the family room with the kitchen, making them look—and function—like one large space. Expanding the kitchen allowed room for a new family-friendly layout, complete with an island work center. At the front end of the family room, French doors lead to the veranda, which widens to ten feet as it stretches across the front of the house, gaining a roomlike feel.

Although doubled in size, the home's original character remains intact. The new space steps back several feet, complementing rather than upstaging the main structure. A columned veranda helps blend old and new while providing bonus space for family gatherings.

BEFORE

One of the new spaces gained by expanding the house sideways is a window-lined breakfast nook that's large enough to seat the whole family for informal dining. Transoms above the windows and limestone tiles on the floor enhance the room's outgoing personality.

Small Additions, Big Gains

In this 60-year-old ranch in Northern California, the right amount of space for daily living and gracious entertaining was already under roof—almost. Two modest-size bump-outs, one on each side of the house, plus a major reshuffling of rooms and walls, dispatched the home's deficiencies nicely.

One bump-out allowed the formal dining room to shift sideways several feet and gain a tall window wall, freeing up space in the middle of the house for a columned center hall. On the other side of the house, a second bump-out nudges the breakfast nook out a few feet, helping to open up a long rectangular area next to the hall and the stairwell. This area, which had been chopped into five different spaces by a maze of interior partitions, became the new kitchen/family room.

At one end, an island work center directs traffic and simplifies casual entertaining, and at the other a hearthside sitting area invites family and guests to linger near the fire and keep the cooks company. Although the two bump-outs added less than a hundred square feet, the house now seems ten times bigger, brighter, and more livable.

When the dining room was bumped out, its ceiling was popped up three feet to make room for transoms above the new French doors. Light from this wall of glass spills deep into the center of the house through the columned arches that define the central hallway.

To make more room for the kitchen/family room, the back hall was shifted to the other side of the staircase. It now aligns with one side of the new center hall, which features built-in storage units and twin sets of columns (one set is structural; the other is decorative).

Tall windows line the breakfast-nook bump-out, pumping light into the new family room/kitchen. A beam above the island indicates where one of the partitions was ripped out to create this free-flowing family gathering space.

MAKE A PLAN

Don't overlook the ceiling when you are contemplating ways to add character and personality to your home. You can add a simple treatment by covering the surface throughout with beaded board or introduce more elaborate details such as vaults, beams, and exposed structures which make the space feel larger than it actually is. You can also add to the height or drop the existing ceiling.

Adding Up

Ripping the roof off your house and adding a whole new level on top may sound like a rather drastic means of gaining more space, but there are various kinds of situations in which it makes a great deal of sense. In some cases, it can be a real moneysaver; in others, the real payback is something you can't put a price on: the ability to stay put and continue calling home the neighborhood that you've lived in for many years or to continue enjoying a setting that you know could never be duplicated elsewhere if you had to relocate.

Three basic options

There are at least three different ways to expand vertically. One is to literally tear off the roof and build a whole new upper level from scratch. Another is to sever the existing roof around the edges and lift it off temporarily, then swing it back in place after the new level has been framed in. A third tactic is to expand an upper level out across an existing one-story section, such as a flat-roof garage or porch.

Get on top of costs

If you need to add a sizable amount of space (several rooms, rather than just one or two) but are faced with a super-tight budget, adding up may be your smartest option. One reason is that you won't have to do any foundation work—one of the more costly portions of any remodeling project—because you'll be building entirely on your existing foundation. (You'll need to have it checked, however, to make sure it can support the additional weight.)

Second, you may be able to save a bundle on roof construction by lifting off the existing roof with a crane in one or two large sections and then reinstalling it on the new second story. Renting a crane is expensive, but much cheaper than building a whole new roof from scratch.

Third, adding a new level that fits on top of your home's existing footprint means you'll be doubling its square footage in a matter of days (the length of time needed to frame up and "weather-in" an upper level). After that, you can finish off the new spaces all at once or one by one, as your budget allows, and if you're handy, you might be able to do most of this work yourself. If the new rooms are simple spaces and if you use relatively inexpensive finishes, the total cost for this type of addition can be about half that of a conventional ground-level addition of the same size.

Embrace your neighborhood

For many families, location is everything. As the country's metro areas sprawl and the cost of buildable land skyrockets, the convenience and charm of a well-established neighborhood often become irreplaceable at any price. If you have little or no room to expand laterally but dread the idea of selling out and hunting for a new neighborhood that feels as homey as the one you're in now, consider staying put and expanding vertically instead.

Even if your remodeling plans are more elaborate than simply adding raw square footage as cheaply as possible, creating a much larger house within the same footprint can net considerable benefits—financial as well as personal. In highly desirable older neighborhoods, a house that doubles in size is likely to double—or triple—in value much faster than those in some of the newer, less convenient areas.

This particularly tends to be true of one-story homes that gain a new second level and make a more substantial or striking architectural statement when viewed from the street. But often the intangible benefits are the real reward. How do you put a price on being able to look out your rear windows at the backyard where your children once played in the lawn sprinkler, or at the huge shade tree that you planted with your own hands when you first moved in? Or knowing that every time you go to the local market or drugstore the shopkeepers will know you by name?

Other reasons to add up

Expanding vertically makes sense if your lot is small and you want to preserve as much open space outdoors as possible for gardening, outdoor living, or simply an adequate sense of separation from neighbors. Or your yard may include some landscape features

you don't want to give up, such as a grand old shade tree, a tall hedge, or a picturesque wisteria-draped pergola. If your family is experiencing growing pains, adding up is a good way to create extra privacy for the kids or for Mom and Dad, and it's also an opportune time to give the main floor of the house some extra stretch by making the walls several inches taller before adding the new level, and by merging or annexing smaller rooms that will no longer be needed downstairs for sleeping when the new upstairs is done.

Adding a full second story may be the least expensive way to double the living area of a small, boxy, one-story house because it doesn't require costly foundation work. Including a front porch in the design keeps the new two-story height from looking top-heavy.

SOLVE DESIGN HURDLES ON SECOND-STORY ADDITIONS

Avoid awkward massing—Doubling the height of a plain, rectangular house can create a boxy effect. Use roof pitches, overhangs, porches, and trim details to offset this effect.

Deal with height restrictions—Local codes may restrict the height of ridgelines for houses in your neighborhood. Check with your city hall before hiring a designer to draw up the plans.

Provide adequate structural support—Some types of foundations aren't strong enough to support a multilevel structure. Also, rafters in a one-story house usually aren't strong enough to double as floor joists for a second story. Have a structural engineer evaluate your home's foundation and framing before you begin planning the new level.

Avoid awkward fenestration—Window size, shape, and placement in the new second story should be coordinated with that of the existing story so that openings line up or form pleasing patterns on each exterior wall from top to bottom.

Maintain pleasing proportions—Skimpy proportions that are not noticeable on small one-story houses are often detracting when such houses double in size. Keep the individual elements of your house—such as windows, trim, eaves, shutters, columns, and dormers—in proportion with its new overall size by beefing them up and/or giving them extra visual emphasis (accent colors, contrasting finishes, etc.).

Rethinking the Ranch

Each of the dormers is almost a room in itself, with display niches in each side wall for special mementos. Larger niches house open shelves in the kneewalls under the eaves.

Two of the new bedrooms upstairs share a Jack-and-Jill bathroom that features twin vanities, a tub/shower alcove, and its own dormer window. The third bedroom has a private shower bath.

Although its shape—a 1¾-story structure flanked by single-story wings—is a familiar one in older neighborhoods across the country, this commodious family home began life as a one-story ranch. To gain more room without gobbling up big chunks of play space in the front and rear yards, the owners converted their screened porch into a family room and added second-floor sleeping areas above the middle portion of the house.

The new space upstairs includes bedrooms for the couple's four young children, freeing downstairs bedrooms for a TV/work space and a crafts room. This domino effect also impacted other public areas on the main floor, which were reconfigured and reassigned to reflect a more informal, flexible lifestyle than the one the original ranch layout had served. The old living/dining area became a multipurpose space that switches roles according to need, mostly a hearth room but occasionally a formal dining room. The kitchen was gutted and retrofitted to accommodate family participation and entertaining, not just one-cook meal preparation.

On the main floor, the old screen porch became a family room. An unusual truss system featuring metal tension rods gives this space architectural "wow" while allowing optimum floor space for family activities.

Three large dormers scoop light into the new second story that now tops this 50-year-old ranch in suburban Chicago. Raising the roof only partway and adding a trellised entry helped keep the street side from looking too massive.

Living It Up Out Back

To gain enough space for a well-appointed master bath, the master bedroom was kept simple and spare. Most of the storage is built into a large walk-in closet that was carved out of an existing upstairs bedroom.

Tight siting on a busy street limited the owners-architects' options for creating oases of peace and privacy upstairs and down in this West Coast two-story. Their solution: convert a pair of main-floor bedrooms in the rear-facing, one-story portion of the house into a family room, and top the new family room with a master retreat. While they were at it, they shuffled existing walls on both floors of the house, which had been converted to a duplex. This yielded a much simpler traffic scheme; a roomier, more workable kitchen on the main floor; and a large multipurpose area upstairs. The rear wall of the house bumped out two feet to give the new spaces comfier proportions inside and to create easy access to the backyard—something the house had totally lacked before.

BEFORE

Deep overhangs, tall
double-hung windows,
and wide trim help merge
old and new on the
exterior. French doors in
the bumped-out wall of
the family room open
to a flagstone terrace.
Upstairs, a roof
deck adjoins the
master bedroom.

Building an Annex

Putting new space under the same roof as the rest of your house isn't always the best or the only option. Building an annex might be a simpler or more effective way to get the kind of extra flexibility you're after. Some annexes are freestanding; others are semi-detached, linked to the house by a deck, terrace, bridge, or other covered passageway.

Examples of structures that commonly function as annexes include garages, sheds, garden pavilions, and self-contained living quarters. An annex may occupy a portion of the structure, such as the attic space above a garage or the indoor half of a garden pavilion, or it may include the entire structure.

Privacy plus

One of the chief advantages of an annex is privacy. In a household where solitude is a rare commodity, creating an oasis away from the house may be the only way to ensure real peace and quiet when you really need it. The degree of separation offered by annexes makes them particularly suitable for spaces that call for an extra measure of privacy, such as guest quarters, a home office, or an apartment for live-in relatives.

Annexes also are good options for spaces that need extra noise buffering, such as teen lounges, kids' playrooms, and rooms for practicing on musical instruments. Another advantage is minimal—or no—alteration of your home's existing roofscape, exterior walls, room layout, or supply of natural light and views. Because an annex is mostly or totally freestanding, it won't require changing your home's roof pitch, giving up windows, or rerouting household traffic. All you may need to change is the shape of your deck or terrace or the location of plants, shrubs, or paths in your landscape.

A place apart

The design of a freestanding or semide-tached structure needn't be quite as conventional as a fully attached structure because it's more a part of the landscape than of the house proper. Therefore, annexes offer an opportunity to escape the relative formality of "regular" shelter and indulge in a bit of architectural whimsy by incorporating visually playful elements like picturesque window shapes, lattice screens, and arbor-style roof structures. Some annexes even function primarily as at-home getaways—spaces tucked away in the backyard or perched beside a pool or patio that capture the feel of someplace even more remote, such as a cabin in the woods.

Trade-offs

One disadvantage of annexes is that you have to extend utility lines beyond the house in order to provide the new space with basic services such as heating, cooling, lights, and running water. This can be costly but the added convenience—or lack of other options—might be worth it.

Another obstacle to consider when building an annex is the set of codes that regulate the design and location in residential areas, especially when used as a separate living unit. In many communities, separate units aren't allowed in areas zoned single-family residential, so you may need to apply for a variance if you include a kitchen and a bathroom in your annex. But annexes can offset these drawbacks by freeing up part of the main house and multiplying space.

This poolside structure provides the space needed for pool equipment storage and serves as a changing room with a half bath. The structure also screens the pool area from the view of a side street.

Hardworking Wing

A semidetached annex helps take the pressure off family spaces in this two-story Colonial in Massachusetts. Part of a one-story expansion across the rear of the house, the annex provides space for a fitness center where family members can work out on exercise equipment while listening to their favorite music—without disturbing the rest of the household. A covered breezeway links the annex to the new mudroom entry. Together they form an angled mini wing that doubles as a privacy buffer, screening the yard from nearby neighbors and the street. They also serve as a handsome gateway to the backyard, which gets heavy use as an outdoor entertainment area for frequent gatherings of the clan.

Inside the annex, large double-hung windows on two walls provide good cross ventilation. Black linoleum tiles on the floor hide scuff marks from gym shoes and heavy equipment.

BEFORE

This semidetached annex angles off one end of a single-story family room/kitchen addition. Its roof pops up a few feet higher to make room for large-scale exercise equipment. French doors open wide to let in plenty of fresh air during workouts.

At-Home Hideaway

Most people reach their weekend getaway spots by pulling out of the garage and heading for a busy highway. For the owner of this detached annex in Michigan, the garage *is* the getaway. One bay of the garage wasn't needed for cars, so it became a breezy backyard retreat that offers laid-back lake-cabin relaxation just a few short steps from the buttoned-up formality of city living.

Created on a shoestring budget with mostly do-it-yourself skills, the 10×25-foot space features a comfy sitting/sleeping area at one end and a wall-to-wall potting bench at the other. Twin windows replace the overhead garage door up front, and a row of tall screened openings along one side provide sweeping views of the rear lawn and garden. The rest of the garage remains intact, so the getaway space is barely noticeable to passersby, which gives it the added allure of a "secret" hideaway.

From the street, this annex is barely noticeable, tucked into a corner next to the remaining two garage bays. Flowering annuals in containers and a window box help soften the old driveway approach near the gate.

Simple finishes give this backyard annex its rustic lake-cabin feel: exposed rafters overhead, 1×6 pine paneling on the walls, and a stained-concrete floor. The seating group includes a daybed for impromptu "sleep-overs."

Assessing Your Situation

To make sure your dream takes shape, real-world factors need to guide your planning early on.

Once you've chosen a basic strategy for your project, it's wise to step back and get a feel for your situation before moving ahead. The addition you've dreamed about will much more likely become a reality if you temper your dreams at this early stage with a healthy dose of practical stock-taking—personal and circumstantial as well as financial. Even the most carefully planned and skillfully managed projects encounter setbacks of one kind or another, but if you begin on a solid footing and have a clear idea of the strengths and options you can use to help you through the rough spots, you'll triumph in the end. Also, if there are serious setbacks lurking ahead, it's much easier to deal with them if you know about them in advance.

Cultivate flexibility

No remodeling project of any size ever turns out exactly as planned, and every project includes at least a few minor setbacks or unexpected complications. Therefore, you'll need to keep an open mind and be ready to think of your dream in terms of alternatives rather than as a single inevitable result.

Get down to business

Home remodeling is very much a reality-based, reality-driven industry, and most of the people you'll be dealing with—designers, builders, subcontractors, inspectors, etc.—spend their days making things work in the real world. Therefore, the sooner you're able to temper your dreams with real-life considerations, the sooner you and your project will be taken seriously by those you've enlisted to help make it happen, and the easier it will be to communicate with them and feel that you are all aiming for the same goal.

Real-world considerations usually rule out an addition like this new front entry bump-out. The footprints of most houses begin at the front setback line, making further expansion toward the street illegal.

Basic Design Determinants

The real world of boards, bricks, pipes, and wires has a way of dictating how your dreams will take shape when you add on. Knowing what these realities are ahead of time will save you costly backtracking once your project begins.

Plate heights

A plate is the 2×4 or 2×6 that runs along the top of a wall. Standard plate height is 8 feet from the floor. When you add on, you'll want the plate height of the new space to match that of your existing walls so that the floors and the tops of windows and doors on each level will match up throughout. If the

plate heights in your house are taller than 8 feet, your windows and doors may also be taller, and you'll want to choose windows and doors for the new space accordingly.

Stair runs

Recently, the height of a residential stair riser has been lowered slightly (from 7 to 6½ inches). During this same period, taller ceilings (above 8 feet) have gained popularity. These factors have dictated longer stair runs, which affect room sizes and floor plan layouts. Old stairwells normally stretched 12 feet end to end (9 feet for treads plus 3 feet for a landing). Under the new standards, stairwells must be at least two or three feet longer. If your addition includes a stairwell, check to make sure you have room to fit the extra length inside your construction footprint. If not, consider using a stair design that turns, doubles back, or borrows existing floor space.

Structural spans

Ordinary milled lumber (2×8s, 2×10s, or 2×12s) are used for spans from 10 to 15 feet. Using these kinds of framing members for longer spans will result in floors that shake, wobble, or sag. If your plans call for an unusually large space, you may need to support the floor with specially engineered wood joists, or with steel I-beams, and you may need to support the ceiling and roof with some sort of truss system instead of conventional joists and rafters.

Pipes, ducts, and stacks

Waste lines in plumbing systems must be vented through the roof via vent stacks—pipes that need a vertical path inside a wall or dead space from the trap to the roof. Making walls line up vertically floor-to-floor to create this path is tricky. Ductwork poses an additional challenge. For optimum operating efficiency, HVAC equipment installed in a central location requires a centrally located vertical path for the flue. This affects floor plan design on each level.

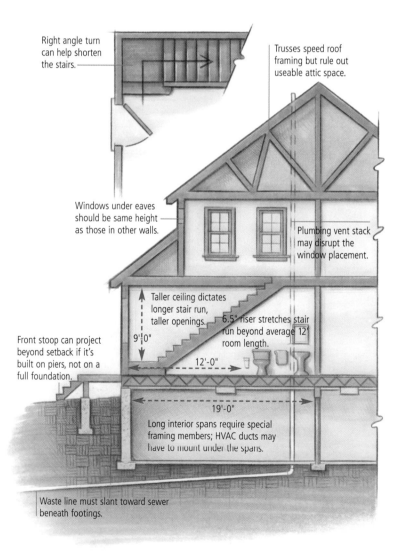

Right angle turn can help shorten the stairs.

Trusses speed roof framing but rule out useable attic space.

Windows under eaves should be same height as those in other walls.

Plumbing vent stack may disrupt the window placement.

Taller ceiling dictates longer stair run, taller openings.

6.5" riser stretches stair run beyond average room length.

9'-0"

12'-0"

12'

Front stoop can project beyond setback if it's built on piers, not on a full foundation.

19'-0"

Long interior spans require special framing members; HVAC ducts may have to mount under the spans.

Waste line must slant toward sewer beneath footings.

Site Considerations

Perhaps the most important set of factors to consider before drawing up a set of plans is the configuration of your site. Although your lot may look virtually identical to your neighbor's, each is unique in ways that could affect the design of an addition.

Topography

Since your house was built, the ground around it may have settled, or construction or landscaping on adjoining properties may have altered the grade near your lot lines, changing the drainage pattern. Adding on could create a drainage trap—thus turning part of your yard into a pond during heavy rains or diverting runoff back toward your foundation. For building sites that are quite steep, grade pressure or sharp drop-offs often call for a special type of foundation, such as reinforced-concrete piers, or basement walls that are beefed up with extra pilasters or buttresses.

Soil Conditions

The subsoil beneath most residential yards is usually quite suitable for construction. Every region of the country, however, has numerous areas where the substrata are either unstable, excessively rocky, laced with natural springs, or subject to sinkholes. A few areas may even be former landfills that haven't yet settled properly. Problem areas like these can cause flooded basements or cracked foundations or require extremely costly construction alternatives. You may want to take a few core samples of the subsoil and have the samples analyzed by a soils lab. Also, check your yard for water leaching out of the ground—an indication that you may have underground springs.

View versus privacy

If the views from your new addition are attractive, you'll want to make the most of them. If not, you'll need to figure out how to screen them. Also, adding on may make you more visible, because part of your living space will project out into the yard in full view of neighbors. Somehow the design will need to strike a balance between preserving privacy, capturing ample daylight, and presenting a friendly face to neighbors.

Access

On some sites, access for heavy-duty excavating machinery, large lifting devices (cranes), and extensive concrete pours can be a problem. If the addition is in the rear and there's not enough room between your house and the neighbors' property for a backhoe and a dump truck, the footings or basement for your addition may need to be excavated by hand—a costly and time-consuming process. In some situations, a crane can be brought in to lift heavy or extremely large loads clear over the house, but trees and utility wires may block the way, or the crane may need to park in your driveway for several days during that phase of construction.

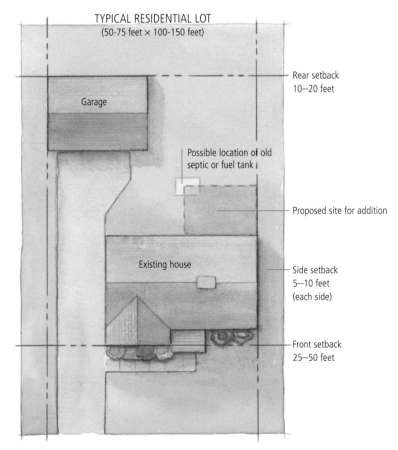

TYPICAL RESIDENTIAL LOT
(50-75 feet × 100-150 feet)

Garage

Possible location of old septic or fuel tank

Existing house

Rear setback 10—20 feet

Proposed site for addition

Side setback 5—10 feet (each side)

Front setback 25—50 feet

Site-Savvy Strategies

The addition to the rear of this 1960s two-story home near Washington, D.C., had to address three distinct challenges posed by the site. First, the house had been shoehorned into one corner of a triangular lot, close to an angled setback line. Second, the rear wall of the house faced directly toward a neighbor's tall privacy fence, not toward the grassy open area in the wide part of the triangle. Third, the sliver of land near the point in the triangle sloped downward from the neighbor's property, channeling runoff between the house and the fence.

Turning these drawbacks to advantages enabled the designer to achieve maximum stretch in the tight space between house and setback line. The corners of the addition were clipped, allowing the new room to jut outward as far as possible without protruding beyond the setback line. Between the setback and the lot lines, the designer added a terrace, a low planter, and a pergola to offset the blankness of the privacy fence and create an inviting outdoor retreat. The terrace incorporates a built-in drainage system that sends runoff to the storm sewer before it has a chance to turn the yard into a soggy bog. Finally, he filled one of the family room's angled walls with tall windows, French doors, and gracefully arched transoms to orient the new room toward the yard's open area.

Clipped corners let the new breakfast nook angle outward along the setback line to form a sunny bay. One wall of the bay angles inward, forming a sheltered area to access the adjoining terrace.

Floor-to-ceiling glass in one of the family room's angled walls shifts the room's main focal point sideways towards the big open area outdoors. Where the yard narrows, a mostly solid fireplace wall provides privacy from neighbors.

Once rendered useless by poor drainage, the 14-foot-wide setback area is now an inviting terrace surfaced with bluestone pavers and topped with a glare-tempering pergola.

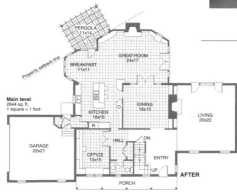

Angled walls in the plan align with the setback, allowing the addition to be several feet deeper. The kitchen was reworked and merged with the new space to form one big family gathering area.

Common Problem Areas

INSPECTION CHECKLIST	ACCEPTABLE	UNACCEPTABLE
Foundation/Basement Condition		
Water damage		
Insect/termites		
Settling/crumbling		
Bowing/heaving		
Rotting		
Cracks		
Siding		
Discoloring		
Deterioration/damage		
Roof Condition		
Flashing		
Gutters		
Vents		
Sagging/dipping		
Chimney Condition		
Masonry		
Liner and cap		
Attic Condition		
Water damage		
Rafters		
Insulation		
Windows Condition		
Frames		
Glass		
Sills		
Doors Condition		
Frame		
Threshold		
Trim Condition		
Deterioration/damage		
Plumbing Condition		
Sagging, leaking, patched pipes		
Water pressure		
Drains adequately		
Fixtures		
Electrical Condition		
Wiring		
Fuse box		
Outlets		
Heating/Cooling Condition		
Odors or fumes		
Sealed and insulated ducts		
Odd noises		
Interior Rooms Condition		
Water damage		
Signs of fire		
Bulging or bowed walls		
Level, firm floors		
Fixtures		

Even if you give careful consideration to basic design determinants and whatever challenges your site may pose, it's likely that your project will hit a few snags once you're under way. Knowing ahead of time what to watch for may not head off snags, but at least it will help you take them in stride and perhaps also build a little cushion into your budget to cover any extra costs they're likely to entail.

Structural deficiencies

As a general rule, there are two types of situations in which structural problems crop up as part of an addition project. One type involves additions that rest on an existing foundation. Examples include bump-outs, upper-story additions, and ones that replace existing extensions (such as a porch, garage, or storage shed).

Bump-outs put extra stress on one particular section of a foundation. If the material used to build the foundation is in poor shape or if the ground underneath it is unstable, cracking or heaving could occur. One remedy is to add piers outside to help support the extra weight. Another is to reinforce the foundation with steel bars or rods. Some single-story homes and most types of extensions are built on concrete pads with shallow footings around the perimeter. This kind of system isn't designed to handle the extra weight of an upper story. Where houses are concerned, substituting stronger footings isn't a practical solution; a more sensible strategy is to add a post-and-beam system to support the upper level independently. As for extensions, it's usually necessary to remove the old footings altogether and build a proper foundation from scratch.

The other common type of structural problem involves floor framing for upper level additions. The ceilings in many single-story homes are framed with 2×6 or 2×8 joists that, depending on the span, can support themselves plus drywall and insulation but may not be strong enough to support an upper floor without bouncing or sagging. The simplest remedy is to "sister in" additional joists to beef up the system before the subfloor for the new level is laid.

Outdated wiring

Adding on nearly always requires adding new circuits to your home's electrical system, and often includes upgrading the lighting, appliances, and other electrical equipment throughout the house. Unless your system has been updated recently, you probably will need to boost its capacity to handle the increased power load. Any new cable and receptacles you install will need to meet current safety standards, and while you're at it, it's a good idea to bring the entire system up to code.

Inadequate mechanical

If you're adding only one or two rooms and if your furnace and air-conditioner are relatively new, your existing mechanical system may be able to handle the extra load. A sizable addition or an older, less responsive system is another matter; you will probably require either a second, separate system that's sized and dedicated to the new space, or a total upgrade that can handle both the existing space and the addition.

Hazardous materials

If your house is more than 25 years old, it may contain materials or substances that require special handling during demolition—either safe removal or permanent stabilization (sealing or isolating). One example is lead-based paint, used extensively until the early 1970s. Particularly

hazardous to small children, fine particles of this paint, if absorbed in the bloodstream in significant quantities, can cause irreversible brain damage. During and after removal of lead-painted surfaces, the house must be thoroughly ventilated and vacuumed. Another example is asbestos. A cancer-causing fiber, asbestos was used in numerous types of construction products from the 1940s through the 1960s. Examples include insulation, ceiling and floor tile, roofing materials, and certain kinds of wallboard paneling. Removal requires special equipment and protective clothing plus total evacuation of the house for several days to prevent inhalation of airborne fibers.

Other potential problems

Before moving ahead with planning, zero in on any other problems that might develop once you begin construction. The best way to track them down is to give your house a thorough checkup ahead of time. Compile an area-by-area checklist like the one on the facing page, then examine and rate each area yourself or hire a professional home inspector to do the job for you. (If you decide to handle this task on your own, be sure to wear protective clothing, including gloves and safety goggles, and keep a respirator handy to guard against breathing asbestos fibers, old paint dust, and other toxins.)

Legal Requirements

Your neighborhood probably is subject to legal constraints. Before you begin the design phase of your project, be sure to check with city and county offices to see what kinds of restrictions are in effect regarding your property. Now is a good time to reread the fine print in your deed and abstract for the property.

Setback restrictions

The legally buildable portion of your lot doesn't stretch to the lot lines; instead, it occupies a "bubble" of space that sits several feet within the lines on all sides. Thus, your buildable area is subject to a front setback, a rear setback, and two side setbacks. The purpose of these inner boundaries is twofold: to ensure adequate open space between neighboring structures for fire safety reasons, and to maintain a uniform streetscape and therefore establish and maintain the street's basic sense of place. On some lots, the bubble is further reduced by easements. Easements preserve strips of open space on private property in order to provide occasional access for non-private purposes. An example is an easement along one side of a lot that abuts a utility trunk line at the rear; the easement ensures legal access from the street for servicing or repairing the trunk line. Because easements often fall inside setback lines, it's important to know if any are in force on your property before you break ground; if your addition should encroach on an easement, you would have to demolish the illegal portion of the structure, which may mean reconfiguring the entire project.

Building area ratios

In many communities, the buildable bubble on each lot is reduced even further by something called a buildable area ratio (B.A.R.) ordinance. Essentially, B.A.R.s set a maximum allowable ratio for the total amount of built space versus unbuilt (open) space within the bubble. This ratio varies from community to community, with typical ratios ranging from 5:10 to 7:10. In other words, if for some reason you wanted to build an addition that enclosed all but a few square feet of your backyard, it's unlikely that local ordinances would allow it. Again, the reasons for such a restriction have to do partly with public safety and partly with maintaining the character and livability of the neighborhood.

Height restrictions

If you're planning to build up, or if part of your addition will tower over your house or that of your neighbors, be sure to check with local authorities regarding rules governing the height of new structures in your area. Such rules serve several purposes: to ensure that ladders on fire trucks can reach the upper floors of residences in an emergency, to maintain a uniform sense of scale or streetscape, to protect view rights of nearby residents, or to preserve access to direct sun for adjoining property owners.

Special requirements

Every region of the country has at least a few communities where unusual rules or limits have been adopted because of unusual local conditions or circumstances. One example of such measures is an ordinance that protects the character of historical neighborhoods. Another is a set of covenants (special agreements or standards) that establish and maintain a particular architectural theme throughout a neighborhood or town. There are ordinances that prohibit on-street parking and limit the number of vehicles that can be parked within sight of the street—a rule that might cause concern if your addition will displace your garage or a big chunk of your driveway. Communities in areas prone to forest fires have adopted codes that specify the type of roofing material you can use, and structures in areas that are subject to frequent tremors must satisfy special codes that make buildings extra resistant to wracking, shifting, and swaying.

Corner Stretch

This remodeled ranch in California offers numerous lessons for expanding on a tight, narrow corner lot. Adding up nearly doubled its square footage, and a couple of strategic bump-outs boosted its living area even further—giving it more depth and character out front. Local height restrictions prohibited adding a third level, but subtle design ploys helped maximize the extra roominess gained by going up and out as far as possible. The main room features a vaulted ceiling with a balcony that opens from the new master suite upstairs. Angled walls and a curved stairwell help carve the new space into the right number of rooms while keeping them from feeling cramped or boxy. On the main level, the bump-outs add stretch to the dining room at one end of the house and create a sunny breakfast nook at the other end.

Big windows and arched transoms give this corner house a friendly face from all angles. An interplay of eaves and gables merges the main floor with the new second-floor addition.

Minimal partitions and vaulted ceilings net maximum spatial drama in the family gathering areas. A wide arch lets the kitchen share views of the hearth; the curved balcony directly above opens from the master suite.

Financing Options

When it comes to financing a new addition, there are several financing options to choose from. It often becomes a matter of simply choosing the one you feel most comfortable with. Here's a look at some of the more common alternatives, plus a few of the hurdles you might need to clear in order to work out a deal with a lender.

Tap your equity

If you have lived in your house for several years and/or made a substantial down payment when you purchased it, you probably could finance your addition partly or entirely with a home improvement loan. Keep in mind, however, that home improvement loans are not mortgages; they are consumer debts, which means the interest you pay on them isn't tax deductible and may be calculated at a higher rate.

Swing a second

If you don't have any major monthly payments other than for your mortgage, there may be room in your budget to make payments on a second mortgage. Compared to home improvement loans, second mortgages impose stricter rules regarding late payments, but the interest rate is closer to that of a primary mortgage and the interest charges are tax deductible.

Refinance

One other alternative is to combine your current mortgage balance and the cost of the new addition into a new, larger mortgage. There are several distinct advantages to this strategy. First, the application process includes a revaluation of your property, which means your borrowing power will automatically increase if the value of your home has risen since it was last valuated (probably at the time of purchase). Second, if your timing is opportune, you may be able to get a much lower interest rate on the new mortgage, which means you'll end up paying less in the long run for the original financial package and you'll be able to make a lower monthly payment on the new package or pay it off in a shorter time. Third, all your interest payments will be tax deductible, and fourth, you'll have one mortgage payment each month instead of two.

Pay as you go

If you'd rather not take on a large monthly debt obligation, and if you have a healthy cash flow plus sufficient assets (other than your house) to use as collateral, you may be able to finance the entire project with a construction loan or make several lump-sum payments over a period of a few months (however long it takes to build the addition). A construction loan is a special account you set up with a lender (usually a bank) for a set amount equal to the cost estimate provided by your contractor.

Review your rating

Before talking to lenders, contact one of the three national credit reporting agencies (see box, see *page 69*) and request an updated copy of your credit report. Check it thoroughly to make sure it is correct and current. If you find any discrepancies, report them immediately to the agency and request a clarification or correction.

Equity in a well-maintained home like this one is an excellent springboard for financing an addition. If the project you have in mind will boost your home's market value without overpricing it for the neighborhood, you may be able to turn a large portion of your equity into ready cash.

Dollars Versus Design

Swinging the right kind of financial package for your project is a key step in the planning process, but equally important is making sure that the money gets spent wisely. Keeping a level head will help, but you also need to take a look at how basic decisions made early in the design process can affect the bottom line.

Cost-conscious shapes

Plain rectangular forms may not seem as exciting visually as ones that curve, angle, swoop, and jog, but they're far less costly to build. Jogs add corners, which in turn multiply labor and materials costs. Compared to straight, flat surfaces, curved and angled ones take more time to lay out and to finish smoothly. This doesn't necessarily mean that you should avoid interesting shapes altogether, or that plain shapes invariably look boring. A good designer will know how to generate architectural oomph with simple, clean lines and planes that are both easy and inexpensive to build.

Space, style, or livability

The three main things you buy with your building dollars are space, style, and livability. How you design the project will dictate how your money gets spent, and that in turn will determine how much of each thing you'll gain when the project is completed. If yours is a fast-growing household that's starved for space and privacy, you'll want to build as much usable square footage as you can afford, and you should be willing to forego a lot of fancy flourishes and fittings—and just-for-looks spaces—to achieve this goal. On the other hand, if you're an empty nester who's ready to invest in and appreciate fine craftsmanship and luxury conveniences, you should be less concerned about adding raw square feet and more concerned about what you can build into each square inch. Make sure your designer knows which category fits you best; that way, your

building dollars are more likely to get spent on the things you really want.

Resale value

Although you may be planning to live in your house for many more years, it's wise to consider what affect the addition will have on the property's resale value. As noted earlier, lenders factor in resale value when reviewing loan applications, and they are likely to reject an application if the design includes changes that would make the property hard to sell in the local housing market. Also, life is always full of uncertainties; you never know when unforeseen events will lead you in a different direction, prompting you to pack up and move. What helps or hinders resale value depends on a number of factors, including the price range, the size of the house, and the region of the country for the property in question. In the affordable ($100,000–$200,000) and mid-priced ($200,000–$350,000) ranges, adding basic spaces such as a third bedroom, a second bath, or a main-floor family room is a more marketable strategy than adding an elaborately outfitted home office or craft studio. In the luxury range (over $350,000), the reverse may be true. Your primary concern is to add the kind of space that you know will give you and your family good value, and it's a well-known fact that recouping your total investment is rare no matter what type of space you add. But it's smart nevertheless to keep one eye on the market as you make key design decisions and to aim for a happy balance between marketability and family goals.

CREDIT REPORTING AGENCIES

Contact any of these three agencies to obtain a copy of your credit report:

Equifax Credit Information Services, Inc.	**TransUnion Credit Bureau**	**Experian**
P.O. Box 740241	Consumer Disclosure Center	P.O. Box 2104
Atlanta, GA 30374	P.O. Box 1000	Allen, TX 75013
800/685-1111	Chester, PA 19022	888/397-3742
	800/888-4213	

Dollar-Stretching Design

The surest way to avoid runaway budgets when adding on is to plug clever cost cutters into every aspect of the design. This expanded cottage in Seattle is brimming with ideas large and small, indoors and outdoors, for making its building dollars work extra hard.

The original one-story structure, which measured a mere 750 square feet, contained two tiny bedrooms, one bath, and a 63-square-foot kitchen. It's now more than twice as big, thanks to a second-story add-up plus a kitchen/family room addition out back. Simple rectangular shapes in both additions helped keep construction costs under control while maximizing the amount of space gained. To avoid a boxy feel, several of the new spaces were topped with vaulted ceilings and gable transoms—a less expensive method of achieving architectural drama than adding extra corners and elaborate millwork. Careful placement of the stairwell minimized hall space, allowing more room for bedrooms and baths on the upper level.

As the "new" house took shape, every detail of the design was studied carefully to determine where additional savings could be incorporated—and where it made sense to invest strategic splurges. Budget-friendly stock cabinets were used in lieu of custom units, plywood siding instead of wood shakes or cedar lap siding, and vinyl casement windows instead of wood double-hungs. Cost-cutters like these left room in the budget for several high-style splurges, including hardwood strip flooring and a granite-topped island in the kitchen/family room, and a whirlpool tub and separate shower in the master suite. The payoff? The house is already worth more than the original value plus the cost of the two additions.

Pricey finishes were used sparingly in the master bath, where tumbled-marble tiles form a border at wainscot height. Less-expensive ceramics were selected for the vanity countertop.

MAKE A PLAN

Building wisely isn't just about economizing; it's also about using your building dollars for best effect. It's smart to invest in quality products that offer durability or timeless style, such as in windows and hard-surface flooring. Or, put your money into something you'll use and appreciate every day such as a richly paneled entry door or silky-action kitchen faucet handles.

In the family room, regular-size window units are clustered to create the effect of a window "wall." Hardwood flooring ties the new space to the existing house and adds an air of timeless quality.

A vaulted ceiling and a transom in the gable wall lend budget-minded style and drama to the master suite. Keeping costs down allowed the owners to splurge on a balcony and French doors that take in a view of Mount Ranier.

Muntins make this newly expanded home's casement windows look like double-hung units—at a fraction of the cost. Low-cost exterior claddings include two types of plywood plus exterior-grade drywall in the porch ceiling.

BEFORE

Shaping the Design

To give shape to your ideas, try picturing how they'll look, feel, and live in three dimensions.

Once you've zeroed in on a particular construction strategy and have your situation well in hand, you're ready to start the design phase in earnest. It's at this stage that your dream actually will begin to gain a definite shape inside and out. Whether or not you intend to rely on the skills of a professional to draw up the blueprints, you'll want to provide substantial input at this stage to make sure the result will be a good fit for you and your family. Good design requires good communication between designer and client, which means numerous meetings at which you review sketches, preliminary drawings, and lists of specifications, and make decisions about various design issues—large and small. As you pore over the drawings, keep in mind that a great floor plan is just one part of the package; think also about how the design will look and feel in three dimensions. Also, try to focus primarily on basic elements of form and style such as room dimensions, ceiling heights, and window shapes and placement. Finishing touches are important but it's easy to get sidetracked by small details that are best addressed later after the shaping process is complete.

Eye-pleasing shapes transformed the front of this once-plain brick ranch in North Carolina. Handsomely proportioned gables cap the new porch and main entry and gently curved arches and buttresses add friendly flair.

Stretching Space

Adding on provides an opportunity to make space work harder and deliver more visual punch per square foot. One way to make this happen is to create extra stretch—the sense that a given room is bigger than its actual dimensions.

Grand openings

There are numerous strategies you can use for achieving this kind of effect. One of the simplest is to include large windows that visually "annex" outdoor space and capture generous doses of natural light. Window areas that are sized and positioned to frame scenic views do a particularly good job of extending a room's boundaries.

Fewer walls

Another simple ploy is to minimize interior partitions so that rooms can share space visually—and even functionally. Wide archways, glass doors, half walls, cutouts, and room dividers are just a few design alternatives you can use instead of solid walls. Although most involve an additional cost, the extra spaciousness you gain is usually well worth the expense. Some room dividers are elements you may be planning to include anyway, such as a fireplace or a stairwell.

Taller ceilings

A third common strategy is to raise the ceiling height. An extra-tall room feels spacious

Adding an open-beam second story above this living room made its horizontal dimensions seem almost twice as large. The extra height also allowed room for a soaring wall of glass, merging the indoor space with the great outdoors.

even when the horizontal dimensions are quite modest. Even if you boost the height only two or three inches, the result can have a subtle psychological effect, making people feel like the room is more comfortable without realizing why. Keep in mind, that extra-tall ceilings work best for large or active-use rooms; in small, intimate spaces, they sometimes seem less inviting. Also, taller ceilings (higher than the standard 8 feet) require careful planning because they affect numerous other elements of the design, such as the heights of doors and windows, the rise and run of a staircase, the length of wall studs, and the size of panels used for interior and exterior finishes.

Additional space tricks

Other space stretchers you may consider include lowering the floor level a few inches (and thus effectively raising the ceiling height); adopting a clean, simple finishing scheme; and using color and artificial light to make the walls or ceilings look farther away than they really are. Spare detailing creates an air of spaciousness, whereas elaborate detailing "eats up" space and may make the room feel crowded. Pale-color surfaces or those washed with light appear farther away or less solid—pleasant effects to strive for in small rooms where it's not practical to add actual inches to the wall height.

A simple cutout pass-through keeps this modest-size kitchen and dining room from feeling boxed in. Both rooms share light and views through the windows and rear door, and simple detailing in each room maintains a spacious, uncluttered look.

Wow Power

Although this interior is dramatically open and contemporary, the exterior blends well by echoing the roof pitch, window styles, and siding of the original structure. High-rise walls with windows that reach floor to ceiling turn this simple rectangular room into a pavilion of light. Natural-finish flooring provides visual anchorage and sets off the white-upholstered furnishings and white area rug.

The footprint for this 18×21-foot sunroom addition is a simple rectangle, yet the room itself packs a visual punch powerful enough to stop you in your tracks. It owes its "wow" power chiefly to a combo of clever space-stretching ploys that turn what might have been a featureless, boxy space into the home's architectural centerpiece.

At least two of the space stretchers are obvious the moment you step into the room: a soaring ceiling and a handsomely scaled Palladian window wall. The ceiling's extra reach offers contrast to the other rooms in the house, all of which adhere to the 8-foot-high standard that typifies suburban Colonial-style design. The window scoops

in a panoramic view of trees and a nearby river, stretching the room's horizon into the landscape. Less obvious, but nonetheless important to the overall spatial effect, is the fact that the floor sits several steps below that of the existing house, further amplifying the height of the ceiling.

Large beams hidden in the ceiling let space flow freely between the sunroom and the kitchen. A ziggurat-style banister stops short of the ceiling to maintain the sense of spatial flow.

Light Fantastic

Once a ground-hugging ranch, this East-coast country house now sports the classic style of an old Colonial waterfront cottage. A taller roofscape, a rambling veranda, and a gracefully arched entry portico played key roles in the transformation.

Typical of most 1950s ranches, the interior spaces of this home felt hemmed in by flat ceilings, blank walls, and conventional-style window and door openings. Giving it a roomier feel involved a relatively modest amount of stretch: a steeper roof pitch plus a small bump-out and a screened porch addition out back. Deft reshaping of the existing spaces netted the most dramatic changes. Flat ceilings in the main room gave way to 18-foot-high vaults that capitalize on the taller roofscape. Dormers punctuate the vaults, funneling in extra daylight to showcase the room's new reach.

A wall separating the old entry and dining area was replaced with a pair of cabinets, creating dramatic through-views from the front door to the backyard. The wall that isolated the kitchen made shrunk to an island work center, merging the kitchen and former dining room into an airy family gathering space. Bigger window areas out back, including the new bump-out dining bay, open up the whole house to its lush setting, which includes magnificent old shade trees bordering a large pond.

A large bay of floor-to-ceiling glass encloses the bump-out dining space at the back of the house—and frame a view that can be seen from the front door.

MAKE A PLAN

Bay windows are addition favorites, usually used in kitchens, dining rooms, or eating areas to add style and natural light. Because a bay window is three-sided, it provides a wide sill that is an excellent place for light-loving plants to thrive. In living rooms, bays can also be used to make room for window seats.

Arched transoms, wide sidelights, and a gracefully curving barrel-vault ceiling give the front entry a new roominess and casual elegance. A pair of cabinets help define the entry area while preserving its informal, open feel.

Solving Traffic Problems

This breakfast nook tucks into a window-lined corner of a kitchen bump-out, just off the beaten path between the back door and the front hall, and within arm's reach of the range and the island. Banquette seating under the windows helps prevent crowding in the main circulation area.

Before the design of your project begins to take on a definite shape and room layout, think about how your family interacts with the spaces you have now—where the main traffic routes are, where bottlenecks occur, where extra steps are needed, and which living spaces are forced to do double duty as halls or entry foyers. As you begin planning the addition, watch for opportunities to incorporate solutions to these traffic problems.

Mapping the routes

Take a close look at the main traffic routes in your house. Do the circulation spaces (halls, stairwells, connecting rooms) provide easy access between quiet and active areas and between outdoor and indoor living areas? Is the heaviest traffic zone in a convenient location, one that can easily handle wear and tear and keep noise and bustle contained? If so, will the addition help or hinder this flow? Maybe your project needs to include a new whole-house circulation scheme, one that relocates the high-traffic zone, reverses the stair landings, and/or shifts the central hall to a new position (or creates a central hall or entry area where one was lacking).

Removing roadblocks

Most any home that's several decades old is likely to contain a few elements that work against the day-to-day routine of today's families. Common examples are dead-end kitchen work spaces that were designed for one-cook food preparation, and formal dining rooms that force you to skirt three sides of the dining table to get from the living room or the front entry to the kitchen. The result is bottlenecks, rush-hour traffic jams, physical isolation, and needless extra steps. Adding on presents an opportunity to loosen up the circulation scheme by merging spaces, eliminating rooms that no longer have meaning for today's lifestyles, and shifting activity areas outward to make room for alternate paths and for more convenient connecting spaces (halls, landings, traffic lanes, transition spaces) in the middle of the house.

Adding traffic "directors"

If your addition will include a hall, stairwell, landing, or vestibule, or a room that will have a traffic lane along its perimeter, consider incorporating features that direct traffic by defining these areas visually (but not necessarily isolating them). Half walls or walls with large cutouts do a good job of segregating traffic lanes from living space. So do freestanding built-ins, such as storage units, island work centers, or display shelves. Another effective option is a decorative screen made of louvered or glass panels or some type of fretwork. Even a row of slim columns will do the job, creating a psychological boundary while letting space and light—and social interaction—flow freely.

Service Plus

Pushing out the rear wall of this kitchen netted far more than a much-needed dose of extra elbow-room. It also worked out some major traffic problems; the layout had been crisscrossed by multiple traffic lanes and plagued by awkward corners and jogs and dueling doors—surefire traffic snarlers. The addition houses a new breakfast bay plus an expanded service entry that positions the basement stairs closer to the back door. The new layout, 3 feet longer than the old one, consolidates the fixtures and appliances within an elongated L, with a long, slim island serving as a traffic buffer. The island also works as a staging area for the breakfast nook and the adjoining formal dining room, allowing cook's helpers to clear and serve without having to invade the main work triangle.

Family-Friendly Layout

Several major problems plagued the layout of this vintage home's active living areas. The only informal gathering space was a boxy breakfast nook measuring just 8×6 feet. The kitchen work triangle straddled the main path between the back door and the stairs to the bedrooms and basement. And chopped-up wall areas in the kitchen necessitated a hodgepodge storage and appliance layout, generating extra steps to perform the simplest tasks. Annexing 9 feet of the backyard netted room to relocate the kitchen, the rear entry, and the breakfast nook, and convert the old kitchen to a cozy hearth room. Reshuffling the activity areas generated a more livable traffic

pattern. The kitchen work area is now segregated from—yet still handy to—the main route to and from the back door. And the stairs to the bedrooms lead directly from the new family gathering room and the enlarged breakfast space.

Expanding and relocating the kitchen allowed room for an island cooking center that overlooks the new hearth room and eating area. Also, there's now more wall space for appliances and storage units.

Relocating the walk-in closet and pushing out one wall several feet opened up this bathroom to a whole new dimension of space, light, and convenience.

Two-Way Bath/Dressing

This master bath originally measured just 8-feet square—no bigger than the closet that adjoined it. Besides being too cramped

The reworked plan allows traffic to flow smoothly around the walk-in closet rather than bunch up inside it. Boosting the square footage netted room for twin vanities plus a makeup table and a toilet compartment.

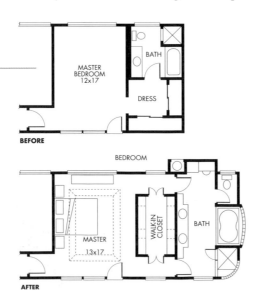

BATH

MASTER
BEDROOM
12x17

DRESS

BEFORE

BEDROOM

WALK-IN
CLOSET

BATH

MASTER
13x17

AFTER

for two people to use the space at the same time, it was also a traffic deadend—one door in, the same door out. Bottlenecks and elbow-bumping during morning rush hours were unavoidable. Expanding outward another 8 feet accommodated an open-ended traffic scheme and a spacious two-person layout. The walk-in closet was moved inboard and given a double entry, freeing exterior wall space for a whirlpool tub alcove and large, sit-down shower enclosure. Short corridors at each end of the bathroom connect to the bedroom and the closet, eliminating collision-prone traffic even during the busiest part of the day.

Direct Approach

Finding the front door of this two-story cottage in Oregon used to be quite a challenge; it was hidden behind the chimney, facing away from the street. Once inside, you had to thread your way through a maze of halls and rooms to reach the kitchen and family room. The same maze was the only route between those rooms and the stairway to the bedrooms. Several savvy tweakings remedied these and other glitches in the floor plan. One end of the dining room became the foyer for a new street-side entry. Walls came down to merge spaces and create simpler, more direct routes between entries, stairwell, and family gathering areas. An angled breezeway linking the house and the garage became a mudroom, taking some of the traffic pressure away from the formal entry.

The new front entry tucks into a sheltered area next to the kitchen. Generous-size columns and an airy trellis frame the front door and sidelights, extending a warm welcome to visitors while making the entry area easy to spot from the street.

Blending Old with New

At this early stage in the planning process, it's easy to get excited about adding new spaces and to forget about creating a seamless fit with what's already there. Making new and old look like they belong together doesn't happen by accident; it requires some key decisionmaking up front, a sensitive handling of design details, and an unwavering determination to invest extra time, money, and/or effort to get just the result you're after. Without such planning, your builder's only option is to make the exterior and interior of your addition look totally standard—as if it were a piece of stand-alone new-home construction.

Which look fits your game plan?

A true blend of old and new should result in a "meant-to-be" look—that is, the addition that your house seems to have been waiting for all along. If that's your aim, then you'll need to decide how far you're willing to go to achieve it. Do you want a perfect match between old and new, or would you be willing to settle for a harmonious blend? Which option you choose depends on your aesthetic tastes, the degree to which you'll be able to ride herd on that part of the project, and the amount of wiggle room you have in your budget. Perfect-match design can be pricey, even if your existing house is only a few

decades old, and can cost a veritable fortune for much older homes. But anything is feasible if money is no object. Harmonious blends are more affordable because they simply echo the design of the original structure rather than duplicate it faithfully, and they rely more on stock products and materials rather than custom-fabricated goods. A seasoned designer knows how to incorporate such echoes so that old and new look compatible without sending your budget into a tailspin.

Do a little research

Even if you'll be relying mainly on professional talent to achieve the blend you're after, it's a good idea to play an active role in this part of the design process. Besides learning about your home's architectural heritage, you may be able to provide your designer with an extra set of eyes—and legs—for tracking down hard-to-find products that complement or amplify that heritage.

Do some smart shopping

Whether your objective is a perfect match or a harmonious blend, your designer's general aim will be to create a consistent look throughout, so that nothing—not even the smallest details like drawer pulls or faucet handles—will cause a jarring note by departing from the primary stylistic theme. Such consistency is far easier to achieve today than it was a few decades ago, thanks to the wide range of vintage-style products now available. But it also entails a great many more decisions along the way. Of course, you may find this process fascinating, especially if it includes researching and preserving your home's architectural character. You may even prefer to do much of the product shopping yourself, poring over catalogs and brochures and surfing the Internet for the perfect pieces to complete your look. What for some is a burdensome chore is for others a labor of love.

Although this Cape Cod cottage had always lacked a covered entry, its new portico seems to fit in perfectly. The addition's simple, classic lines and well-proportioned columns and coach lights help give it that "meant-to-be" look.

Borrowings from the Craftsman era turn this recently built entry hall into a pleasing blend of old and new. The dark oak door and newels were custom-crafted to set the tone; lighter-scaled trim and light-toned wood flooring strike a more modern note.

ARCHITECTURAL ROOTS

Below is a list of resources that may help you determine which architectural style best fits your existing house.

Publications:

• *A Field Guide to American Houses*, by Virginia and Lee McAlester (Alfred A. Knopf, Inc., 1984)

• *American Homes: An Illustrated Encyclopedia of Domestic Architecture*, by Lester Walker (Black Dog and Leventhal, 1981)

• *American Houses: A Field Guide to the Architecture of the Home*, by Gerald Foster (Houghton Mifflin, 2004)

• *American House Styles: A Concise Guide*, by John Milnes Baker (W.W. Norton, 1994)

Organizations:

• National Trust for Historic Preservation, 1785 Massachusetts Ave., NW, Washington, DC 20036-2117

• Historic American Buildings Survey, National Park Service, Department of the Interior,1849 "C" Street, NW (2270) Washington, DC 20240-0001

Websites:

• www.realviews.com—Outlines the development of American home styles from Georgian to Foursquare.

•http://jan.ucc.nau.edu/~twp/architecture/—A guide to architecture styles throughout the United States.

Design Dos and Donts

BAD
- Disproportionate shape
- Haphazard windows
- Looming side wall
- Unrelated siding material

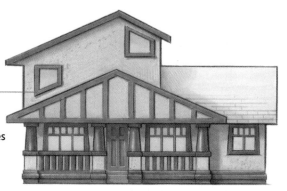

BETTER
- Matching roof pitches
- Friendlier profile
- Strange window shapes

BEST
- Matching roof pitches
- Well-integrated profile
- Harmonious window shapes
- Matching siding material

Ineptly designed additions tend to fall into at least one of three categories: "mismatched," "unneighborly," or "temporary," with the worst examples scoring high in all three categories. Knowing what kinds of design no-nos characterize each category, and taking care to eliminate them from your own project, will help ensure that your new spaces will achieve that coveted meant-to-be look. Telltale signs of a mismatched addition include haphazard or poorly merged roof planes; awkwardly juxtaposed shapes; and window styles, roofing materials, siding, and other elements that seem totally unrelated to those of the original structure. Traits of an "unneighborly" addition include long, blank, windowless walls facing the side or front setback lines; architectural styling that creates a jarring, out-of-place affect in the streetscape; and tall projections that loom over neighboring homes and block light and views. Traits of a "temporary" design include skimpy proportions; flimsy or cheap surface finishes; and amateurish or hastily constructed foundations, roofs, and appendages (stoops, decks, trellises, etc.). The sketches, *left*, for a second-story addition, illustrate how dramatically the results can vary depending on how much care and attention you give to making the right design choices.

Exactly matching the brickwork, roofing, fascia, lumber dimensions, and other materials in this front-porch addition resulted in a porch that blends smoothly with the 80-year-old home.

Designed to appear original to the 1906 home, this new screen porch echoes the house's rounded dormers and stone detailing. Using the same roofing material and same trim color was also critical to making the addition seamless.

Vintage-Style Products

These antiqued bronze pulls evoke the early 1920s. Other period styles now being offered again include porcelain, clear and colored glass, and pendant or "drop" versions.

As the small sampling on these pages illustrates, today's market offers a wide range of vintage-style products for building and remodeling—everything from neoclassic to Craftsman and from appliances to garage doors. In most categories, vintage-style goods also are available in several different price ranges, from inexpensive, mass-market knock-offs to big-ticket, specialty-item reproductions. As a general rule, however, expect to pay a little more for the period look than for standard-issue designs because extra character usually involves additional detailing, more complex shapes, and/or special finishes. And if you want new items that are equal in quality to the ones that were used when your house was built, you may need to limit your selections to a few choice items in a given category; normally, only the best-grade products are likely to offer the workmanship of yesteryear's standard goods. Also, certain items within a given category may be available by special order because they appeal only to a narrow segment of the market. Again, expect to pay a premium for being this particular.

Although it looks decades old, the millwork in this window seat bump-out, including the fluted newel and Corinthian column, are stock items currently available.

Numerous cabinet manufacturers offer units with vintage-style legs that can give a kitchen an old-fashioned, "unfitted" look.

In this vanity area, old-time character was created by combining several types of vintage-style tiles: a high-relief border, embossed accent tiles, and generous-profile chair rail sections.

WHERE TO GET VINTAGE CHARACTER

• **Catalogs:** Numerous mail-order catalogs offer a wide variety of vintage-style products. Examples include Pottery Barn (888/779-5176), Sundance (800/422-2770), Restoration Hardware (800/762-1005), Historic Outfitters (800/247-4111), and Waterworks (800/899-6757).

• **Websites:** You can shop for period fixtures, fittings, and flourishes on the Web by clicking on such sites as Renovator's Supply (www.ren-sup.com), Architectural Products (www.archpro.com), and Bath and More (www.bathandmore.com).

• **Estate sales:** Often the bargains that get grabbed first at estate and tag sales include old doors, windows, chandeliers, plumbing fixtures, cabinets, and other items being disposed of in order to empty an old house.

• **Salvage demolition companies:** These firms offer salvage materials at bargain prices—or for free—if you're willing to remove the items and haul them away yourself. Treasures to watch for include soapstone countertops, solid oak doors and trim, solid bronze pulls, beveled-glass mirrors, and leaded-glass windows.

Mellow Mix

Unless you look closely, you could easily assume that this brand-new dining room addition dates from the early 1900s. The basic structure, an airy, vaulted space with tall casement windows, owes its mellow character to a strategic mix of vintage-style finishes, fittings, and furnishings. The window and door trim, though it looks late-Victorian, is stock millwork currently available on the market. The tall storage cabinets, also stock items, were "aged" with an antiqued finish and decorative crown molding to create the effect of old-time built-in cupboards. The chandelier, a garage-sale find, is one of the few items in the room that actually dates back nearly a century.

A harmonious blend rather than a perfect match, this period-look kitchen addition gets its yesteryear flavor from budget-friendly finishes such as stock millwork and salvaged door hardware.

MAKE A PLAN

If you plan to install hardwood floors, consider using salvaged wood rather than new wood. Remodelers often look for lumber pulled from old buildings, barns, and gymnasiums to create an aged look. To find salvaged wood, check the Internet or talk to contractors and salvage experts.

Trellises give this sunroom addition the feel of an old-fashioned arbor. Dark-stained beaded-board paneling on the ceiling and an antique wicker seating group amplify the room's period atmosphere.

Trellis Tracery

If the project you have in mind calls for large areas of glass like those in this sunroom addition, blending old and new can be particularly challenging. Here, sliding patio doors form the three exterior walls. To soften their "modern" lines, a series of redwood trellises were mounted on the outside, merging the new space with the picturesque character of the existing house while preserving a breezy, open feel. Arched portions in the trellises create a transom effect between the upright supports. Eventually the glass walls will be further softened by a hanging garden of trumpet vine and clematis on the trellises.

Creating Focal Points

When you add on, each of the new spaces you create will generate a visual impact of some sort by drawing your eye to particular elements as you pass through a space or spend time there. Such elements are called focal points. When reviewing sketches or preliminary plans, think about what things your eye will tend to focus on when you begin using those spaces. Will it be something dramatic, such as a grandly scaled fireplace or view-scooping window wall, or will it be uninviting, such as a blank wall or an all-too-clear view down the hall that serves the children's bathroom?

Design-driven options

Rather than leave such matters to chance, it's best to build in the ones you do want, while the design is still in flux. Several basic types of focal points can easily be incorporated into the design of almost any addition. Some are strictly interior elements, such as a fireplace/media wall or an elegantly detailed staircase. Others are strictly exterior, such as

a view of a garden or a courtyard fountain, or the continuation outside of an interior wall surface, an exposed beam, or a row of columns.

Focal points can work their magic in small spaces as well as large ones. Even a tiny powder room can make a visual statement—usually with a distinctive vanity bowl or decorative mirror. In large spaces, it's tempting either to have too many focal points, all of which compete for attention, or to use elaborate furnishings, accessories, and window treatments as an antidote for architectural emptiness. Neither strategy wears well; the eye tires quickly when overworked. A better strategy is to rely on one major and one subordinate element to anchor and unify the visual experience.

Multipurpose design tools

Although the primary purpose of a focal point is to make space visually interesting, it can serve any of several other purposes at the same time. Some focal points serve as anchors for the room's activities, with the furnishings, lighting scheme, and other key elements oriented accordingly. Examples include hearth areas, media centers, and window walls.

Focal points can be used as visual diversions too. If the view outside isn't worth exploiting, or if the room has no exterior wall, the next best thing is an eye-catching view inside. Often this consists of room-to-room vistas framed by attractive archways, columns, or cutouts. Other common examples include alcoves, bridges, and staircases. Furnishings can serve as focal points too, particularly if the room has been shaped to showcase a certain piece or two that have artful characteristics. An example is an heirloom breakfront that sits within its own sized-to-fit alcove.

Focal points often double as traffic directors or room dividers. Archways are one example; freestanding fireplaces are another. Various types of built-ins qualify also, such as island work centers and modular storage units. So do screenlike partitions that use

At the entrance to this kitchen, a lighted niche turns what might have been an empty passageway into an artful and pleasing composition.

A whirlpool tub makes a logical focal point in a master bathroom. Here, other elements of the room, such as a shower enclosure and a toilet compartment, create an alcove that "stages" the tub platform.

glass panels, open grids, or decorative fret-work to buffer traffic on one side while providing artful relief on the other.

In projects where artful detailing is a key part of the design scheme, focal points can establish or reinforce the main theme of the design. Or, they can repeat or echo design elements from the existing structure, thereby helping to tie the new and the old thematically. If, for example, the windows of your house have a distinctive pattern of leaded-glass panes in the upper sashes, you could incorporate this look in a series of focal points throughout the new spaces—in glass-panel doors, a fretwork screen, an abstract composition of moldings above the fireplace, and so on—and thus tie them all together visually, while giving each one an artful flair all its own.

The vanity area in this master suite becomes a focal point for the bedroom via a glass-panel door, sidelights, and transom, helping to anchor that side of the room and give it a furnished look.

MAKE A PLAN

You may want to consult a lighting designer during the initial planning stages of your remodeling project. A lighting designer can assist you in selecting the right lighting scheme that will illuminate good design and make rooms function better and more efficiently. Check with lighting specialty stores for a professional in your area.

The hefty masonry components in this fireplace help create a visual anchorage that contrasts artfully with large sections of glass in the walls that surround it. The other elements (cross beams, cornices, and window sashes) complement its geometric mass.

Windows and Doors

One trait that sets good home designs apart from amateurish or thoughtless ones is that each face of the structure looks attractive and artful, even the ones facing neighboring houses. Window and door placement plays a key role here. Central air-conditioning systems may make natural ventilation less essential than it once was, but if the shapes, sizes, styles, and locations of windows are determined either purely for utilitarian reasons or by whim, the results will be a mishmash of "holes" punched at random in the exterior walls. And if the walls are more than one story tall, there'll be no sense of order to tie the two levels together. Granted, other variables tend to dictate window and door placement, such as room layouts, household traffic routes, and location of storage areas and built-ins, but a good designer knows how to juggle all these factors and still devise a set of elevations that look organized and artful on the exterior as well as on the interior.

Create artful compositions

You can help achieve this yourself by thinking about each wall of your house as an artistic composition—sort of like an abstract geometric painting. All the elements in the wall—particularly the openings—should relate to each other logically by lining up vertically and horizontally or forming some type of overall pattern that makes them read as integral parts of a whole. Also, the openings (voids) and the solid areas (masses) should balance or complement each other (the most pleasing ratio between voids and masses is roughly 50:50), either in a formal, symmetrical arrangement or in an artfully asymmetric one.

Multiple options

Following guidelines like these is easier than you think, because windows and doors are wonderfully versatile design tools. As you play with exterior and interior wall elevations, keep in mind that openings can be artful as single shapes, as multiple shapes in a decorative composition, or as grand sweeps of transparency that turn your wall into a giant mural. Also, do a little preliminary window shopping—literally—to bring yourself up to speed on the latest design innovations. If you haven't bought new windows or doors lately, you'll be amazed at the range of choices now available—new shapes, new convenience features, new styles, and new standards of performance and durability in virtually every price category.

Windows turn the wall in this breakfast nook into a two-story, wraparound mural. The lower part of the room is rimmed with a banquette; together, the windows and the seating form a unified design.

When placed carefully, a single window can become an artful design element. The vertical lines of this arch-top window balance a long stretch of solid wall on one side of a living area.

Choosing Finishes

Some of the most important decisions you'll be making once your project gets under way have to do with surface treatments—the part of the project you'll actually see and touch every day and the part that will require the most maintenance. There are three fundamental ways to look at surfaces and the kind of finish each should have.

The first is form. Surfaces can be flat, round, zigzag, concave, convex, tilted in, tilted out, stairstepped—the list is nearly limitless. One rule of thumb may help you pare it down quickly: simpler forms are far less costly to build and usually easier to maintain. A smoothly curved lavatory bowl may not be as eye-catching as one that

The layering of several colors on this accent wall creates a subtle patina effect that adds a sense of depth and character. Applying the colors in bold squares suggests a paneled treatment. It also mimics the pattern in the area rug.

ripples, but it will be much easier to keep clean.

A second way to categorize surfaces is in terms of texture or pattern. Again the range is practically limitless, everything from rough and grainy to etched and carved; from tweedy or floral to striped or plain—or a blend of several of these. Keep in mind that texture and pattern can easily be overdone; it's best to aim for a mix that balances or tempers texture or pattern with plainness.

The third way to view surfaces is in terms of color. Although the number of different colors is virtually infinite, certain colors or color groups work better than others for a given type of space (for a few examples, see Subtle Tricks with Color, *page 100*).

Expressions of style

Certain issues or concerns are likely to impact your decisionmaking. The first has to do with the overall look you want to achieve, one that expresses your home's architectural style, for example, or your personal style. If an urbane, formal look is what you're after, you may want to focus on finishes that are sleek, polished, intricately embellished, or classically simple. If rustic informality is more to your liking, you may want to focus on finishes that are rugged, rough-textured, naturally patterned or colored, and simple in the sense of handcrafted or homespun.

Generally the more formal and sophisticated the style is, or the more elaborately it's executed, the more costly the finish and the more time-intensive the work of creating or installing it. If a formal look is what you have in mind, but your budget is tight or you're not prepared to allow your builder generous leeway in getting the project completed, you may want to stick with design concepts that use inexpensive, easy-to-install materials (such as drywall and stock trim) to create an effect of studied simplicity and purity. Likewise, if rustic informality is your thing but budget and time restraints will play a key role, resist the temptation to go all out; re-creating natural charm from scratch (such as a mountain-lodge theme for

a family room) can easily run your budget into the ground and cause your project to bog down with excessive detail work.

Price points

When builders prepare estimates for projects, one of the first questions they ask the homeowner is, "What price point do you have in mind for your project?" Within almost any category of finish product—whether it's siding, countertop surfacing, paint and stain, or hardware—you'll find three basic levels of quality and three basic levels of pricing: "budget" or "affordable," "middle market," and "high-end" or "luxury." Knowing ahead of time which price point best fits your pocketbook and lifestyle will help put you on a solid footing with your designer or builder and will also help narrow the choices when it comes time to pick finish products.

A mosaic-tile tabletop inspired the Mediterranean color scheme of this kitchen. A soft shade of blue on the walls creates a sense of intimacy for the table area and yellow accents echo splashes of tropical sunshine.

Quality and durability

If rock-bottom pricing isn't your sole criterion for making selections, then issues of quality and durability should factor into your thinking. High-quality finishes tend to look and feel more substantial and have richer color. Often, the reason is that they're made with genuine materials rather than synthetic substitutes—although for certain categories of products, the synthetic versions are actually superior. In flooring, for example, natural hardwoods are still superior to synthetic look-alikes, but ceramic tile is, in many respects, a better choice than natural stone.

Quality and durability often go hand in hand, but not always. Certain types of popular, high-end finishes can be high-

maintenance. One example is cedar shake siding, which must be retreated every year or two to maintain color consistency and minimize deterioration. Another is stone countertops, which must be resealed several times a year to prevent staining. When making selections, weigh one factor against the other, depending on where each product will be used and how much time and money you're willing to invest in maintaining it. For exterior finishes it's best to place high priority on minimum upkeep and long-term durability. For certain types of interior finishes, such as cabinet hardware and plumbing fittings, a little extra maintenance might be worth the pleasure you gain from seeing, touching, and admiring those items daily.

The wainscot paneling in this living room looks like a pricey surface treatment but was created by nailing stock trim directly onto drywall. Pale hues work with the wainscot's classic simplicity to give the room an air of serene spaciousness.

SUBTLE TRICKS WITH COLOR

Orange encourages appetites, so some shade of orange is a good color for eating areas. Mauve or purple is the least appetizing color.

Green and blue are the most soothing colors; red is the least soothing.

Yellow suggests sunshine, and is therefore a mood-enhancing color.

Pale colors suggest distance; dark colors suggest closeness and intimacy.

Black reflects little light and therefore obliterates detail, so it's a good choice for camouflaging ugly shapes inexpensively, such as exposed ducts.

Dark green walls give this vanity alcove a sense of intimacy, and high-relief drawer fronts lend a bold sense of form. Matte-finish mosaics in the tile border add subtle texture and pattern.

Walls

For wall treatments, reduce the range of choices for each area by keeping certain selection criteria in mind. Besides price point—always a key concern—judge each product in terms of cleanability, ease of installation (could you do it yourself and cut labor costs?), and suitability for the point of use (some products are poor choices for high-humidity areas such as kitchens, baths, laundries, and basements). Here's a thumbnail comparison of the most common types of treatments.

Paints and stains

One of the least-expensive options ($20-$30 per gallon), painting or staining also requires the least amount of technical skill. Today's paint and stain products are relatively easy to work with; many are formulated for nondrip application, and most are water-based for easy cleanup. Some

are specially formulated for high-moisture areas; others for easy maintenance (look for products labeled "washable" or "scrubbable") and/or long wear.

Wallpaper

Ranging anywhere from $20 to $150 per single roll, wallpaper is roughly as affordable as paint, depending on which product you choose and how much area you need to cover. It requires somewhat more skill than paint or stain, but it is still fairly easy to install. In areas where cleanability is essential (kitchens, baths, mudrooms, nurseries), it's best to use vinyl wallpaper.

Wood paneling

Costs for solid or veneer wood paneling normally range between $10 and $75 per square foot, but extra-fancy millwork or rare species of wood can cost even more. One of the least expensive options is veneer plywood grooved to look like beaded-board or car siding. Another cost-cutting option is panel kits, a product designed for do-it-yourselfers, with most of the millwork and panels precut for quick assembly.

Stone and ceramic tile

Costs in this category range widely, from $1 to $100 per square foot. Glazed ceramic tiles in standard sizes and colors are the least pricey; fancy design or hand-crafted accent tiles made with special molds or cut stone are the costliest. A good way to economize is to use pricey accent pieces sparingly to dress up a lower-cost tile layout. Glazed or porcelain ceramics clean up the easiest; stone tiles are porous and can stain easily, so they need to be re-sealed at least once a year.

Synthetics

A wide variety of synthetic products are available for wall treatments and their costs range from 50 cents to $100 per square foot. Examples include melamine hardboard paneling, fiberglass composite modules (stone and brick look-alikes), solid-surface tiles and sheets, and laminate tiles.

The subtle-textured surfaces on the walls of this dining room were created by applying a thin coat of pigmented plaster over the drywall. This treatment works best for rooms that are softly lit.

Floors

When choosing flooring products, it's important to compare options on the basis of cost, cleanability, and ease of installation. Two other factors for this category should be considered: safety (especially for children and elders) and durability. Sleek-finish products such as glazed tile or highly polished stone or hardwood may be easy to clean but very treacherous for those who are unsteady on their feet. (Slippery surfaces also are poor choices for aging pets.) Deep-pile carpeting, on the other hand, poses a different problem; not only is it hard to clean thoroughly, it also shows footprints, and it impedes wheelchairs and furniture that rolls on casters, such as a desk chair or service cart.

New options

If you haven't shopped for floor surfacings for several years, you'll want to get up to speed on the many new options now available. Some are particularly budget friendly, such as the various types of laminate wood floors (laminate is an economical substitute for solid wood strips or stone tiles). Some are designed to be especially user-friendly, such as frieze carpeting (a low-pile shag look-alike that doesn't show footprints). And a few are old standbys that have been revived in new guise, such as stained or stamped concrete (a brick or stone look-alike) and linoleum (vinyl's forerunner, reissued in updated colors and patterns). Use the chart below as a thumbnail guide to help keep the various options sorted in your mind as you visit flooring showrooms and building centers.

MAKE A PLAN

Laminate floors feature a top layer that is made of the same materials as laminate countertops—but ten times tougher—to help sustain the wear and tear on the floor. There are finishes that mimic a wide variety of wood species.

Flooring Options

MATERIAL	ADVANTAGES	DISADVANTAGES	COSTS
LAMINATE	Durable; can be installed over existing floor; easy to clean; wide range of colors and designs	Cannot be refinished if damaged; can be noisy unless foam underlayment is used	$45–$80 per square yard; professionally installed
CERAMIC TILE	Durable, water and stain-resistant; wide choice of colors, designs, and shapes	Can be cold and noisy; glazed tiles can be slippery when wet; dirt and stains can get into grout if not sealed	$9–$45 per square yard
STONE TILE	Virtually indestructible; easy to clean; withstands high temperatures	Marble is cold and slippery; hard on feet; difficult to repair; glossy surfaces require periodic repolishing	Varies depending on shipping distance; installation prices range $9–$45 per square yard
CONCRETE	Hard-wearing, long-lasting; easy to clean; optimum design flexibility	Prone to staining and cracking; can feel cold and hard on feet; requires periodic resealing	$36–$90 per square foot; stamping and etching boosts cost
HARDWOODS	Wear-resistant; long-lasting; warm, natural look; comfortable underfoot; easy to maintain; can be refinished	Vulnerable to moisture; some woods easily dent; may darken with age; somewhat difficult to repair	$29–$47 per square yard installed
RESILIENT	Comfortable underfoot; easy to maintain; good design flexibility; sound absorbent; sheet goods eliminate seams	Prone to dents and tears; may bubble, buckle, or peel up over time as mastic ages	$10–$38 per square yard for vinyl; $42–$45 for linoleum
CARPET	Slip-resistant; warm and comfortable; sound absorbent; wide range of colors and styles	Absorbs spills and stains; promotes mold and mildew growth; not easy to deep-clean	$5–$95 per square yard, plus $2.50–$6 per square yard for pad

Counters

Granite slabs provide a warm, dressy finish and easy-to-clean surfaces in this contemporary-style kitchen. When countertop and backsplash surfaces are cut from stone, it's best to use simple shapes like the ones shown.

Before kitchens became popular areas for relaxing at home and for entertaining guests, and before master suites included lavishly appointed baths, countertop surfacing was basically a two-product industry: plastic laminate and ceramic tile. Both of these products are still widely used and offer distinct advantages in terms of cost, cleanability, and ease of installation. Of the two, tile is by far the more durable, but it is also more expensive.

Trendy new tops

That was then. This is now. Following the trend toward bigger, warmer, more stylish kitchens and baths (as well as laundries, home offices, and craft studios), countertop manufacturers now offer a wide range of new options. Most are considerably pricier than laminate, partly because all require skilled labor and special tools for installation. Perhaps the best known example is solid surfacing (stonelike slabs or tiles made

with acrylic resins). Less common but gaining popularity every year is honed or polished stone (granite, marble, limestone, slate, or soapstone). Of the two, solid surfacing is the easiest to maintain and offers the greatest design flexibility; stone provides the special appeal of natural colorings plus random graining and veining. One throwback to kitchens of the 1940s, stainless steel, has reappeared as a popular companion material (such as on a large island work center) for kitchens that feature commercial-style appliances and sinks. And an old material that's now being used for residential countertops for the first time is concrete. As you weigh the pros and cons of each, factor in location (cooking, serving, dining, crafts, home office, kids' bath, adult bath, etc.) before making a selection.

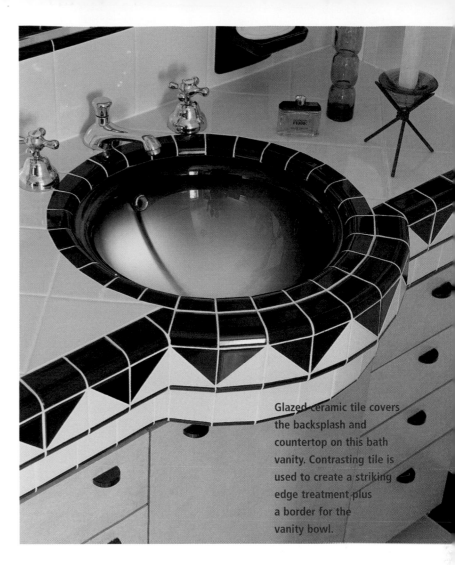

Glazed ceramic tile covers the backsplash and countertop on this bath vanity. Contrasting tile is used to create a striking edge treatment plus a border for the vanity bowl.

Countertop Options

MATERIAL	ADVANTAGES	DISADVANTAGES	COSTS
LAMINATE	Durable; inexpensive; easy to maintain; wide range of colors and designs	Gouges or scratches can't be repaired	$26–$60 per square foot installed
CERAMIC TILE	Durable; water- and stain-resistant; wide choice of colors, textures, and shapes	Moisture and dirt can get into grout joints; unglazed types must be resealed periodically	$18–$90 per linear foot installed
STONE SLAB	Virtually indestructible but requires periodic resealing; withstands high temperatures	Expensive; marble and limestone readily absorb stains and dirt; difficult to repair	$125–$250 per running foot installed
CONCRETE	Hard-wearing, long-lasting; easy to clean; easily adaptable to various shapes and colorings	Prone to staining and cracking; requires regular resealing	$70–$150 per linear foot installed
BUTCHER BLOCK	Wear-resistant; lasts indefinitely; provides a warm, natural look; needs occasional refinishing	Vulnerable to moisture; some woods, such as pine, dent easily; tends to darken with age	$40–$75 per linear foot installed

Exterior

If you want to achieve a perfect match with your existing house, choosing exterior finishes will be simply a matter of looking for the products and materials that come closest to meeting that requirement. Be forewarned, however, that for houses several decades old, exact matches no longer exist for most items. Also, a material's exposure to the elements will have altered the look of certain finishes, such as shingles or wood shakes, so you may need to freshen the exterior color scheme of your entire house in order to achieve a proper blend. In some cases you may be able to disguise discrepancies by salvaging part of the old and by using the new in less-noticeable spots.

Achieving a harmonious blend rather than a close match makes the selection process much easier because you have a much wider range of options. The palette of finishes you put together can echo what's already there or reinterpret it, or it can form the basis for a whole-house facelift.

Decisions, decisions

No matter which goal you pursue, exteriors involve a number of different finish areas—each requiring a particular set of designs and/or product selections to be made. In addition to the two most obvious areas—the exterior walls and the roof—you'll need to make choices regarding window and door trim, soffits, cornices, vents, gutters and downspouts, and the outside face of the foundation. You also may need to deal with railings, columns or posts, porch or deck planking and skirting, ceiling finishes, and outdoor lighting. You'll want to judge the various options in each category on the basis of cost, durability, and ease of installation. See Exterior Cladding Options, *page 109,* for a list of options.

Special considerations

For exterior finishes, there are also some special considerations to factor into your thinking as you make your selections. One

Cedar shingle siding offers a rich palette of texture, pattern, and subtle color variation. Here it's combined with a fieldstone-faced foundation for a warm, rustic look.

Earth-tone hues on this home's exterior play up its Craftsman styling. The three-color paint scheme brings out simple trim details that otherwise would easily be overlooked.

of the most important is ease of maintenance. Low-maintenance finishes play a much more direct role in home design now than they did a few decades ago, because today's families have less time available for repainting, restaining, or residing their houses, and because the number of older homeowners continues to grow every year. Manufacturers have responded by developing new types of low-maintenance products, many of which cost little more than their high-maintenance counterparts.

Another special consideration is point of use. The type of roofing material you choose may depend on what pitch the slope is for that part of your roof (metal roofing can be used on shallow pitches; asphalt or shake shingles need medium or steep pitches). The type or color of wall cladding you choose may depend on which way the wall faces (bright colors tend to fade quickly in direct sun).

A third consideration is architectural suitability. Unless you're aiming for a close match with existing finishes, you'll need to proceed with caution when introducing new ones. Make sure that each design treatment or product you pick will be in scale with your home's architecture and appropriate to its architectural style or period, and that it will relate comfortably with other finishes in the neighborhood—especially those of homes close by.

Cut stone—a relatively pricey cladding material—is used judiciously here as an accent wall, lending heft and presence to the entry porch.

New Trends and Options

The chart, *opposite*, lists a number of exterior finishes that are traditional standards, plus several that are relative newcomers. In the siding category, two materials that already are widely accepted are fiber-cement and synthetic stucco (EIFS). Fiber-cement siding is a blend of wood fibers, cement, and sand that is poured into molds and dried to form boards that resist shrinking, warping, burning, and insect damage. Although it looks like traditional wood siding, it's much more

stable and, therefore, requires considerably less maintenance. Synthetic stucco, used mostly in Sun Belt areas where stucco-and-tile houses have long been a favorite style, consists of a "sandwich" of insulation, fiberglass mesh, and two layers of synthetic coatings that resemble traditional stucco. It's more durable than real stucco (no cracking) and offers more design flexibility.

One of the latest trends in roofing materials is traditional-looking shingles made

with nontraditional substances such as cement, fiberglass, and rubber. Examples include concrete shingles that are textured to look like wood shakes—a smart choice for areas where forest fires are common— and slate-style shingles made with recycled rubber tires. Also, metal roofing—an old standby that normally was applied in sheets—is now available as individual shingles or as shingle panels. Some of the panel versions closely resemble clay tile roofing or slate in overall color, shape, and pattern.

Exterior Cladding Options

MATERIAL	ADVANTAGES	DISADVANTAGES	COST
WOOD BOARD & SHINGLE	Easy to install; natural grains and colors; wide variety of profiles	Requires frequent painting and staining; subject to warping, sagging, dry rot, and insect damage	High
ECONOMY VINYL	Low maintenance; even, stable coloring; quick coverup for problem facades	Limited variety of accessory pieces (trim); limited color choices; tendency to sag in extreme heat	Low
PREMIUM VINYL	Low maintenance; even, stable coloring; high-quality facelift for problem facades	Good variety of accessory pieces; broad choice of colors; stands up well in extreme heat	Moderate
FIBER-CEMENT	Realistic-looking texture and shape; won't warp, buckle, or sag; can be cut with a circular or handsaw	Requires skilled labor for installation; must be painted rather than stained or left natural	High
STEEL	Long-lasting finish; easy upkeep; can be repainted	Limited color choices; dents easily; develops rust spots if chipped or scratched	Moderate
SYNTHETIC STUCCO (EIFS)	Long-lasting finish; easy upkeep; optimum design flexibility; integral color	Can cause major moisture damage if not installed properly	Moderate
BRICK & STONE	Very durable; natural hues, shapes, and textures; easy upkeep	Requires skilled labor for installation; requires special structural support	High
SYNTHETIC STONE	Very durable; natural-looking hues, shapes, and textures	Requires skilled labor for installation	Moderate

Working with the Pros

To turn your dreams into reality with a minimum of stress and strain, rely on a team of well-qualified professionals.

The crisp detailing and quality workmanship in this family room addition are sure signs that an architect and a seasoned general contractor were key members of the project team.

Behind every successful remodeling project stands a group of people who work together as a team, making sure that all the work meets certain standards and that the work is completed at a specified time and in the proper sequence. For most home remodeling projects, the leader of this team is the general contractor. If you plan to manage the project yourself, then you are, in effect, the general contractor. If you don't have time or the necessary practical experience to do this job yourself, you'll need to hire a pro to head up the team.

Either way, your project is likely to involve numerous other team players, including designers, product specifiers, subcontractors, inspectors, and day laborers. You'll need to make legally binding commitments with various members of the team in order to hire their services. It also means that, once the work begins, you and your family will need to interact on a daily basis with strangers under your own roof and to deal day to day with the chaos and inconvenience that normally accompanies a construction project. In this chapter, we'll take a closer look at what's involved, and provide some pointers for keeping things running smoothly—and helping you keep your cool.

Design Checklist

As you meet with architects, designers, government officials, subcontractors, and others, be prepared to answer the questions below. Those you work with will certainly come up with more questions, but knowing these answers will save time as you begin planning.

Your House and Its Occupants

- Style of your house?
- Year it was built?
- Size in square feet?
- Overall dimensions?
- Orientation of the house: North? South? East? West?
- General type of construction: Brick? Wood frame? Other?
- Type of foundation?
- Type of windows?
- Type of roofing material?
- Type of siding?
- Is there a basement?
- How many people live in the house? Will that be changing in the foreseeable future?
- Do you entertain often? Does the present setup of the house accommodate your entertaining requirements?
- Are the sizes of public spaces adequate?
- Do you desire more quiet or privacy?
- Does anyone in your house have special needs?

Building the Addition

- What type of addition do you want?
- To what degree do you expect this to be a do-it-yourself project?
- Who will do the design work?
- Who will construct the project?
- Who will obtain permits?
- What are the setback restrictions of your lot?
- Does your home fall within any other special restrictions, such as those of a historic district or a covenant area?
- Will you supply any materials?
- What is the overall budget?
- How is the project being financed? Bank or lending institution? From savings? Other?

Kitchen Additions

- Who will design the kitchen? A certified kitchen designer? The architect? Another designer? Yourself?
- What will be the style of the cabinetry?
- What cabinet supplier will you use?
- Will the plumbing wall be moved?
- Are you adding appliances that will need 220-volt electric service or any other special lines? What electrical grounding will be necessary?
- Will any walls be removed?
- Do you want additional windows or skylights?
- Are you hiring a lighting designer?
- Do you want additional electric outlets?

Bathroom Additions

- Will the locations of any electrical or plumbing fixtures change?
- Do you want a separate shower and tub?
- Are you adding a jetted tub?
- Does your home need new water or drainpipes?
- Do you need a larger bathroom?
- Do you want additional electric outlets?
- Will the bathroom be located conveniently to serve the bedroom(s)?
- What surface materials do you have in mind: Ceramic tile? Vinyl? Solid surfacing? Stone?

Living Room or Family Room Additions

- Do you want the new room to open onto other rooms?
- Will there be exterior doors? Should they be fully or partially windowed?
- Are you adding a window wall?
- Are you adding a fireplace? Gas or wood? Will you build a hearth area with a mantel?
- What kind of floors do you want: Carpet? Hardwood? Laminate? Ceramic or stone tile? Concrete?

General Design Questions

- What are your favorite colors?
- Does the household gather for meals? What is the breakfast routine? What about dinner? Do you entertain?
- Do you have swatches of fabric, paint color chips, or wallpaper samples that capture the look you desire? Do you need a place to display your collections?

A study now tops the original entry of this home to create a new exterior focal point.

BEFORE

Assembling Your Team

Depending on the scale of your project, your team may need to include some or all of the following key players: a designer or architect; a builder/designer, a general contractor, or a project manager; a landscape architect and/or a landscape contractor; a kitchen designer and/or a cabinet layout planner; and a lighting designer and/or an interior designer. With so many chiefs, who is really the team leader? Again, it depends on the scale of the project. In large, elaborate projects, the architect oversees the entire process and represents your interests in any decision making or dispute-settling situations. In normal-size projects, the architect or designer plays a less prominent role, with the general contractor taking the lead.

Tracking down candidates

One common way to locate good team players is by word of mouth. If someone you know has had a good experience with a certain designer or contractor, you probably will too. Other good sources are home products expositions and model-home tours.

Designers and contractors often exhibit their services at trade shows, and you can see their work firsthand at model home tours and chat with those whose work appeals to you.

Picking the right people

Good teamwork is partly a matter of good chemistry. Look for professionals that you feel comfortable with and who seem to understand and respect the vision and objectives you have in mind for your project. To make sure the people you hire are seasoned and reputable, take time to interview and screen several candidates before making your selections. Check them out with the Better Business Bureau to make sure no complaints have been filed recently by previous clients, vendors, or subcontractors. Check with the Remodelors Council at the local chapter of the Home Builders Association. Also, ask each candidate for references (names of clients for whom they've done similar work).

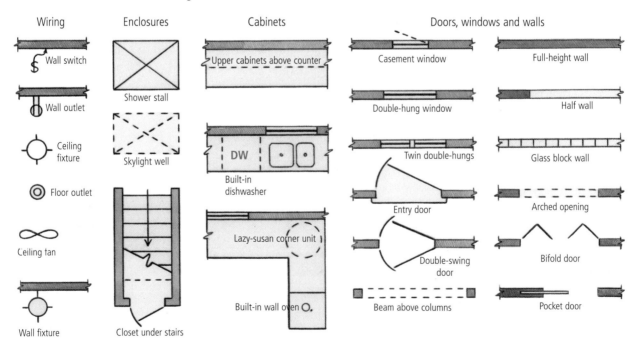

Wiring — Wall switch, Wall outlet, Ceiling fixture, Floor outlet, Ceiling fan, Wall fixture

Enclosures — Shower stall, Skylight well, Closet under stairs

Cabinets — Upper cabinets above counter, Built-in dishwasher (DW), Lazy-susan corner unit, Built-in wall oven

Doors, windows and walls — Casement window, Double-hung window, Twin double-hungs, Entry door, Double-swing door, Beam above columns, Full-height wall, Half wall, Glass block wall, Arched opening, Bifold door, Pocket door

Understanding Contracts

Putting down in black and white the services that each member of the team will perform is an essential step in launching the project, even if the people you're hiring are relatives or close friends. Besides heading off misunderstandings, contracts offer protection against the cost of delays and other kinds of setbacks that sometimes occur during remodeling projects. Although the term "contract" may seem intimidating or overly formal, most construction contracts are relatively short, simple documents written in plain English. It's important to remember, however, that the blueprints (plans) and the specifications (lists of materials) are considered part of the official agreement between the homeowner and contractor and are therefore officially part of the contract. All three documents are therefore legally binding, so any changes made after construction begins must be initialed by you and all other parties to the agreement.

Standard-form agreements

For the written portion of the document, most contractors supply a boilerplate text contract that includes provisions for the following: a work schedule and a payment schedule; statements designating liabilities and insurance coverages in the event of injuries, theft, or damage at the work site; statements that specify where materials will be shipped and who will be responsible for receiving, checking, and warehousing them; and clauses that say the builder cannot be held responsible for delays caused by weather and other forces beyond his or her control.

Even in a boilerplate contract, there should be places to write in various provisions that apply specifically to your project. If not, you should request that such information be attached and initialized by all parties so that you can state whether you'll be obtaining any products or materials yourself (contractors normally make all purchases at wholesale and collect a 15 percent markup), or will be doing any of the work yourself (for which the contractor will need to allow credit).

Custom-drafted agreements

Don't assume that a standard-form text document is trustworthy simply because it looks official; if you're dealing with a stranger and there's any part of the document that you don't understand fully, have your family attorney review it before you sign on the dotted line. Or ask your attorney to draw up a contract from scratch (if you don't mind paying a fee to gain the extra peace of mind this might provide).

LEARNING THE LINGO

Before studying contracts or talking to professional designers, builders, or subcontractors, you may want to bone up on certain terms that are used widely in the construction industry. Here's a sampling:

- **Broom clean:** A legal term that specifies removal of all construction debris from the job site upon completion of the project, including sawdust, packing materials, and leftover construction materials.
- **Allowance:** The standard amount (usually a middle-market figure) that a contractor includes in his or her cost estimate for items that are to be purchased directly by the homeowner (example: lighting fixture allowance).
- **Structural:** A term used to identify any element that is load-bearing, such as a wall, column, or beam. (Some elements that appear to be structural may be decorative.)
- **Punch list:** Items noted by a contractor during his or her final walk-through of the project that need attention before the job can be officially completed.
- **Rough-in:** The first stage of installing a system, such as plumbing or electrical wiring, after rough carpentry is completed.
- **Trim-out:** The final stage of installing a system, after interior finishes are completed. Trim-out includes installing fixtures and fittings and mounting cover plates and decorative trim.
- **Wet wall:** The wall that houses the main water pipes and waste line for a home's plumbing system.

Interacting with the Team

In order for the work to proceed as smoothly as possible, decisions will need to be made quickly as issues arise, and many of these decisions are ones you'll need to make yourself. If you don't, the contractor may be forced to make them for you in order to avoid costly delays. Professionals bring to a project experience and knowledge, and it's only reasonable to give considerable weight to their opinions, but that doesn't mean you should defer to them on every issue or question. Remember that you are the one who will live with the decisions long after the other members of the team have moved on.

Make frequent inspections

Reputable contractors respect fair-minded homeowners who insist on quality work, but it's up to the homeowner to demand that inferior work be torn out and done properly. This means you need to play the role of unofficial inspector. As the work progresses, you should visit the site frequently. Your general contractor can't be everywhere, so an extra set of eyes comes in handy for spotting slip-ups before it's too late—or too costly—to fix them. If you do spot problems, report them to your general contractor; it's his or her job, not yours, to ask the subcontractors to correct any problems involving their work. Also, if, during your walk-through inspections, you find things that you'd like to change, discuss them with the general contractor first; they may involve extra costs for labor and materials, plus documentation in the job contract.

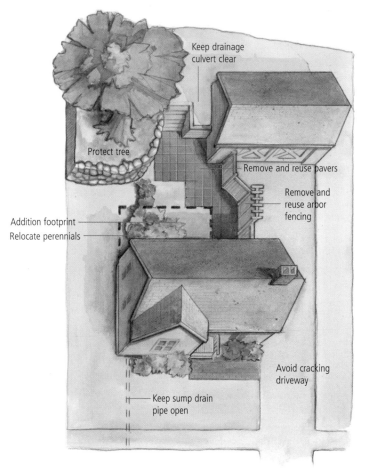

Keep drainage culvert clear

Protect tree

Remove and reuse pavers

Remove and reuse arbor fencing

Addition footprint
Relocate perennials

Avoid cracking driveway

Keep sump drain pipe open

Protecting the Site

Before you meet with your contractor, compile a list of the features on your property that will need to be protected or moved during construction in order to preserve them. Most contractors are willing to honor these requests, but it's important to address the matter early. (Don't assume, for example, that outsiders will know that the ornamental grasses in your dooryard garden aren't just tall weeds.)

Nonmoveable items

Major items on your list should include things that need to be protected in place, such a shrubs, bushes, trees, outbuildings, fences, and arbors. Also list any exterior surface treatments that can't be repaired easily, such as stone or brick veneers for which there are no close-match replacement materials. Add existing paved areas to the list too—particularly if your project will involve heavy machinery or the delivery of heavy loads of materials. If your driveway is likely to crack or settle or if you're fussy about maintaining its appearance, give your contractor fair warning.

If you want to save any plantings or other landscaping features that will be displaced by the addition, remove these items ahead of time. However, if you also want to save the topsoil and reuse it to cover the backfilled areas around the new structure, add this to your list. Topsoil is a valuable commodity, and your contractor should be willing to ensure that it will be removed carefully and stockpiled until it's time to do the finish grading.

Surviving the Mess

Another list you should go over with your contractor before work begins has to do with living day to day in the midst of a construction project. Be ready to accept a certain measure of inconvenience—noise, dirt, and having strangers traipse across your property are par for the course when remodeling—but you needn't give up all rights of privacy and ownership. Setting a few ground rules up front may help prevent friction later.

Roughing it

Most additions involve temporary interruptions of basic services such as water, power, phone, home security, and heating or cooling. Some also involve loss of kitchen, bathroom, or laundry facilities for several days, weeks, or months. Making do with temporary arrangements is largely your responsibility, but your contractor may be willing to schedule subcontractors to minimize service interruptions.

Stroking the neighborhood

Consider also the impact your project may have on your neighbors. Before the work begins, give all the neighbors a heads-up about your project. Knowing in advance

what to expect usually makes it easier to endure the extra noise, dirt, dust, and traffic that accompany a typical construction project. This also gives you a chance to find out ahead of time whether any of your neighbors have special concerns that should be addressed up front before you move ahead with the project.

SAVVY SURVIVAL STRATEGIES

If basic services will temporarily be out of commission while you're adding on, use some of these tactics to keep your household routine humming.

• **Eat out:** Plan to do most of your cooking on a gas grill, and switch to paper plates and other disposables to minimize cleanup chores.

• **Nuke it:** Prepare a series of main dishes ahead of time and store them in the freezer, then thaw out each meal in the microwave.

• **Keep your cool:** Move the refrigerator temporarily to the garage, porch, or basement. Use it to keep perishables and beverages cool.

• **Camp out:** Rent a recreational vehicle and park it in the driveway or backyard to provide temporary kitchen and bathroom facilities.

• **Give yourself a break:** Check into a hotel or motel on the weekends to catch up on baths and showers, and to get away from the noise and mess.

• **Miscellaneous tips:** Buy one or two large plastic waste bins (with lids) to store fresh water; pack up and stow fragile items that might be damaged by dust or vibrations; cover rugs, floors, and furniture with drop cloths to protect them from dust and muddy boots; keep a shop vacuum handy to clean up demolition and construction dirt, pipe leaks, and other large messes.

Fine-Tuning Your Project

Giving the design—and your budget—some extra tweaking will help keep your project headed in the right direction.

Once the general shape of your project comes into focus and you pick the key players for your project team, it's time to shift gears—from establishing broad outlines or directions to developing refinements, adding finesse, and making strategic course corrections. When you bring in the pros, things start to happen quickly. In a matter of weeks, a seasoned designer can turn your napkin doodlings, your wish list, and your scrapbook of ideas into a very real-looking addition on paper. At that point, he or she will begin making suggestions that you may not have considered yet about fine-tuning the design. Some of these suggestions may involve the kinds of things you might have wished later that you'd added anyway, such as energy-efficient windows or a built-in central vacuum system. Others may involve some strategic maneuvering of the budget to make room for a few smart splurges; a real pro will know how to give your building dollars maximum buying power and will have good tips about where to spend bonus bucks.

As you begin the process of fine-tuning, think about what you might do to upgrade your existing house too so that it's more in synch with the addition. Having a crew of skilled laborers on hand offers a great opportunity to get some other work done that may need doing eventually anyway. You might even want to develop a long-range master plan in which the addition and certain related areas are the first phase of an ongoing whole-house update.

Subtle refinements are more effective when they look like integral components rather than afterthoughts. Extra touches in this hearth area, such as the wall sconces, molding details, and leaded-glass windows, are elements that were incorporated into the design at an early stage in order to create a unified whole.

Tap Special Sources

Tracking down just the right finish or flourish for each part of your project can be a challenge because what you're looking for may be too specialized—either one-of-a-kind items or goods that appeal only to a narrow segment of consumers. Yet, finding the perfect product or material is often what makes or breaks a design idea.

Work with your designer

Your design pro will have the credentials that often are needed for opening doors that are otherwise closed to the general public—doors to industry and design showrooms, for example, where limited-market goods (the kind that often have that extra "designer" touch) are available only at wholesale "to the trade." During meetings with your designer, you will likely thumb through thick catalogs of product brochures from such sources. If you do, you'll discover a range of choices far exceeding anything that exists in local shops or home centers.

Some special-source doors are open to the public. Although it's usually not convenient to visit factory showrooms for specialized custom-crafted products—many of which are manufactured in small, out-of-the-way locales—there are other places where merchandise of this kind may be on display, ones that lie along more heavily traveled routes. For example, most large urban areas include a design center—a complex of showrooms where specialty-design merchandise is sold only to the trade but where the public can "window shop." Also, large trade expositions often open their doors to the public on the final day of the show to give consumers a sneak peek at new limited-issue goods that will be hitting the market within a few months. Planning ahead to stop at a design center or catch the last day of a trade expo could save you weeks trying to locate hard-to-find items or companies.

REMODELING PRODUCTS ON THE WEB

Mass-Market Sources

Ceramic tile—American Olean Tile; 800/933-8453; www.americanolean.com

Lighting, hardware—Restoration Hardware; 888/243-9720; www.restorationhardware.com

General remodeling supplies—The Home Depot USA, Inc.; www.homedepot.com

Floor/ceiling surfaces—Armstrong; 800/233-3823; www.armstrong.com

Windows and patio doors—Andersen Windows and Doors; 800/426-4261; www.andersenwindows.com

Niche-Market Sources

Solid bronze hardware—Stone River Bronze; 435/755-8100; www.stoneriverbronze.com

Commercial-style appliances—Viking Range; 888/845-4641; www.vikingrange.com

Skylights, roof windows—Velux America, Inc.; 800/283-2831; www.veluxusa.com

Timber-frame structural systems—Timber Framers Guild; 888/453-0879; www.tfguild.org

Fiber-cement siding—James Hardie Building Products; 866/442-7343; www.jameshardie.com

One-of-a-Kind Sources

Architectural salvage—Bauer Brothers Salvage; 612/521-9492; www.bauersalvage.com

Period-style interior and exterior doors—YesterYear's Vintage Doors & Millwork; 800/787-2001; www.vintagedoors.com

Custom-cut inlaid tile—Crossville Ceramics; 800/221-9093; www.crossvilleinc.com

Custom-order ironwork—Jefferson Mack Metal; 415/550-9328; www.mackmetal.com

Custom inlaid floor designs—Oshkosh Floor Designs; 877/582-9977; www.oshkoshfloors.com

Quality always pays off in the kitchen. Here, well-engineered drawers ensure many years of smooth, sturdy operation and clean-lined good looks.

Click your mouse

If you have a fair idea of what you're looking for, an even easier way to find it is to surf the Web, either by making a general search or by checking out broad-based shopping websites such as e-Bay and Amazon. This is an especially good source if you're seeking one-of-a-kind items or goods that are no longer being marketed or manufactured on a regular basis. All the major building products manufacturers have websites, and so do most small-scale companies. Listings in the box, *opposite,* illustrate the broad range of sites online. If you want a specific type of item and aren't able to spot it for sale on any of the major sites, use the Web's special search engines to do your detective work for you. Besides well-known searchers such as Lycos (www.Lycos.com) and Yahoo (www.yahoo.com), there are other sites like WebCrawler (www.webcrawler.com), Infoseek (www.infoseek.com), and the Internet Sleuth (www.isleuth.com). Dogpile.com searches many browsers at once.

Make Savvy Splurges

In addition to cost-cutting strategies you may already have in mind, your designer may suggest other ways to plan your spending to get the look or features you seek. As you ponder how to spend the extra dollars you'll save, focus on purchases that will yield long-term paybacks.

Things you'll use every day

It's much easier to justify splurging for high-quality goods if you know you'll be using them every day. Marble tile flooring for a formal dining room is a needless expense if you use that space once or twice a year; an inexpensive marble look-alike would be a more sensible choice. On the other hand, kitchen drawer pulls that cost twice or three times as much as ones that look similar but feel flimsier add a subtle sense of richness and quality to routine chores.

Make good first impressions

Generally, paying extra for something primarily because it looks more impressive isn't a wise investment. Exceptions to this rule are items that are highly visible to visitors, items that send visual messages about the way you and your family live, and things that display the amount of interest and care you invest in your home. Examples include entry doors, front-facing window areas, and street-side garage doors. Even items that are visible only up close can make an impression, such as front doorknobs or outdoor light fixtures.

This front-facing garage speaks volumes about the owners' concern for period authenticity and for making their home an asset for the neighborhood.

Things That Make Life Easier

Perhaps the smartest splurges of all are those that reduce or eliminate periodic maintenance, netting you a double payback in the long run—lower costs for upkeep, plus more free time to enjoy life. In recent years, low- and no-maintenance building products have gained hot-button status among homeowners and homebuilders, and the building products industry has responded with an ever-expanding array of options. No-paint windows, lap siding, and trim are now commonplace. And no-rot shake shingles and no-stain deck planking are gaining favor year by year. Usually you have to pay extra for products that offer this kind of maintenance-free longevity, but if you plan to live in the house for many years, you'll recoup your investment several times over in savings on maintenance costs. Also, it will be easier to stay put as you grow older because you won't have to worry about budgeting for expensive upkeep—or trying to handle such burdensome tasks yourself. If low- or no-maintenance products are a high priority on your wish list, make sure your designer or builder knows this up front and selects products accordingly.

Vinyl is a popular siding choice because it's virtually maintenance-free. Also, the color is long-lasting because it's an integral part of the vinyl cladding.

Plan for Upgrades

Whether or not your project will be phase one of a multiphase master plan, you may want to factor in a certain amount of long-range planning as you fine-tune the design. What may seem like overkill construction could save you major construction costs down the road when you're ready to tackle the next phase of your master plan or are simply adding some finishing touches to your current project.

Go high-tech

When adding new space, it's smart to incorporate state-of-the-art technology that can be expanded later to include the whole house. High-tech features that are rapidly becoming "standard equipment" in new construction—such as intercoms, home security systems, whole-house home entertainment systems, and networked home computers—involve complex wiring that's much easier and cheaper to install when the framing is still exposed. With the "brains"

or core of the system installed in the addition, expanding it later to include the whole house will probably be much simpler and less costly than doing the whole project at once at some future date after the framing is covered up.

Allow for add-ons

Certain features on your wish list that don't fit your current construction budget can be added later at modest cost if the design and rough-in work are done now. Special framing needed for a prefab fireplace or a hot tub can be included during rough construction, and the fireplace or tub can then be added later without tearing into walls and floors—a process that often requires replacing the finishes throughout a room, not just the area where the feature is being added.

Adding on is a good time to upgrade with a whole-house home management system. You can install the control center of a basic system in the new space, then extend the system and add new features in stages.

If your addition will include a media wall, be sure to add extra wiring and outlets so that you can add new components easily as they become available. Also consider installing wiring for a whole-house video system.

Plan for Lifestyle Changes

It's smart to fine-tune your project plans so that they anticipate other kinds of major lifestyle changes in the years ahead. As with all types of long-range design strategies, lifestyle-focused planning usually pays multiple benefits by saving extra construction costs down the road. It might even save you the cost—and emotional heartache—of having to trade your present home for one that meets a new set of physical needs or priorities.

Working at home

Unless your house is only a few years old, it was built when few people worked at home and retirees rarely pursued second careers. Today's technology makes it much easier to gear up for work at home, either for extra income or to pursue academic goals. If your house lacks a dedicated space (ideally a separate room) for doing work at home, or if the workspace you have needs upgrading or supplementing, you may want to fine-tune your project plans by outfitting some of the new space for a home office or by recycling some existing space for this purpose. Even if you don't need a fully equipped work area yet, it's smart to install the basics during construction, while carpenters and electricians are on site and the inside of your walls are still easily accessible. A well-equipped work station requires extra electrical wiring—multiple outlets, preferably on a separate circuit that's protected from electrical surges—plus a telephone modem, a cable- or satellite-TV connection or separate phone lines for data and voice communication, glare-free lighting, and adequate noise buffering.

Aging in place

Will your house keep pace with certain physical trade-offs that inevitably come with old age? Adding on provides an excellent opportunity to make your home elder-friendly ahead of time. Even if you restrict this type of planning to one particular part of the new space, at least you will have the option of staying put no matter how incapacitated you become in your later years.

Labeled "universal" or "accessible" by industry experts and product manufacturers, elder-friendly design makes especially good sense in the three areas of the house where basic functions of living take place: the kitchen, the bathroom, and the laundry. Making these areas wheelchair-accessible, and making the equipment and built-ins in these areas easy and safe for older hands and eyes to use, is fundamental to any plan that addresses aging as an important design determinant.

Incorporating certain general features of universal design can make the rest of the house elder-friendly too. Examples include lever-style door latches (easier to operate than those you have to twist), wider doorways and halls (for wheelchair access), low-pile or hard-surface floor coverings (for easier wheelchair movement), and ramps instead of steps (for barrier-free wheelchair, walker, and other assisted-mobility movement).

Accomplishing these types of goals is much easier than it was just a decade ago. Many designers specialize in this type of planning and a wide array of new products

A dedicated-space home office like this one can serve as the heart of a networked home computer system, with satellite terminals stationed in various rooms of the house and interconnected via cables hidden in the walls.

are now available nationwide. Several mail-order catalog companies offer a full line of universal-design building products (check the Web for listings under "universal design" or "accessible design"). Also, some major manufacturers of kitchen, bath, and laundry products (appliances and/or cabinetry) offer separate universal-design collections.

Accessible and stylish

If you thought that universal design must look institutional, think again. This master bathroom, *below*, proves it needn't be so. Its lean lines and rich blend of urbane finishes combine to make a style statement worthy of the most sophisticated tastes. A closer look reveals cleverly integrated features that make daily bathing and grooming activities comfortable and convenient for any age—from nine to ninety. There's ample floor space for one or two people to move about whether they're ambulatory or need some type of assistance. The vanity countertops (*not shown*) are broad and deep, offering plenty of parking space at convenient height for toi-

letries and other grooming aids. reach. Glass blocks form the window and part of the shower enclosure, filtering and diffusing natural light to reduce glare while preserving privacy, and close-fitting, limestone tiles provide a smooth, even floor surface for wheelchairs or unsteady feet.

This built-in microwave is positioned at eye level for a seated person, making it accessible to someone who moves about the kitchen in a wheelchair.

There's no curb or step to pose a barrier in the doorway to this shower, and the enclosure is large enough for two people.

Build It Healthy

Outside

■ **Vapor barriers** When installed correctly and coupled with proper mechanical ventilation equipment, vapor barriers help promote indoor air quality by preventing moisture and pollutants from seeping in. They also reduce drafts, thereby cutting energy consumption.

■ **Non-VOC products** Pressure-treated building products contain volatile organic compounds (VOCs) such as formaldehyde, which can leach out over time and may pose a health hazard to those who suffer prolonged exposure. Untreated, kiln-dried lumber, steel studs and joists, and plastic-impregnated wood composite planks are some of the many alternatives that qualify as non-VOC materials.

Place windows on multiple walls in as many rooms as possible to provide for natural ventilation.

■ **Healthy siting** Poor drainage and leaky basements can lead to hazardous mold and mildew growth inside the walls or on interior surfaces. Proper siting is one way to head off these problems. Make sure your addition won't disrupt natural drainage patterns on your property. If you're concerned about groundwater drainage, consider building your addition on a well-ventilated crawlspace foundation, a concrete slab, or on piers instead. Other good measures include adding a layer of plastic sheeting under the basement floor slab and installing a dehumidification system.

■ **Sealed foundation with ventilation** Check to see if basements in your neighborhood or locale are prone to exposure to radon gas, a proven cause of cancer (for specific data on radon-prone locales, visit www.epa.gov/radon/zonemap.html). If you live in a high-radon area, you may want to rule out below-grade living space in your planning, and you may also want to install a special radon-venting system in your existing basement.

■ **Cross ventilation** The exterior envelope of a new house or addition is built much tighter than those of a few decades ago. This results in lower exchanges of indoor air per hour. To ensure adequate natural ventilation (a more earth-friendly remedy than mechanical systems), it's best to go with a floor plan that allows windows on at least two walls in all the main rooms.

Recycled materials

Many exterior finishes are made with recycled materials or byproducts (green materials), which helps conserve resources. The manufacture of some of these products also uses less energy and/or produces fewer pollutants, thus helping to protect the environment. Examples of these materials include slate-style shingles made from ground-up quarry waste, driveway pavers made with recycled rubber tires, and masonry veneers made with pulverized stone chips.

Inside

■ **Paints with low or no VOC** Unlike conventional oil- and water-base paints, the "green" versions are practically odorless and contain very small amounts of chemical fumes that outgas quickly after application.

■ **Solid-wood or UF-free products** Glues and binders used in the manufacture of many cabinets, furniture frames, and structural and decorative panels contain urea formaldehyde (UF), which outgases VOCs. Look for solid-wood or UF-free alternatives.

■ **Sealed-combustion gas appliances** Pilot lights on conventional gas-fired appliances, such as stoves, water heaters, and gas fireplaces, continuously release small amounts of carbon monoxide, not all of which escapes to the outdoors through vent pipes. To avoid buildup (a special concern in extra-tight houses), install sealed units that use outdoor air for combustion, or an electronic spark for ignition instead of pilot lights.

■ **Water-filtration system** Urban growth is threatening the availability of clean water sources for metropolitan treatment facilities. Build in extra precautions against pollutants by installing point-of-use filtration equipment (undercounter or faucet-mounted), or invest in a whole-house filtration system.

■ **Hard-surface flooring** Wall-to-wall carpeting, long a popular and inexpensive floor covering, can become a trap for dust, mold, pet dander, and other tiny particles that trigger allergic reactions in some people. Area rugs that can be removed easily for periodic cleaning are a much healthier option.

■ **Low-voltage lighting** Conventional lighting systems use line-voltage wiring and incandescent lamps (bulbs), which waste energy by producing heat as well as light. In low-voltage systems, a transformer steps the voltage down, and special types of bulbs (such as fluorescent or halogen) convert most of the energy to light.

■ **Recycled materials** Help the planet stay healthy by choosing indoor products that contain recycled materials. Options include tile made with pulverized glass, cabinets made with finely shredded straw, and carpeting made from recycled plastic milk jugs.

Hardwood floors are a healthy alternative to wall-to-wall carpet that can trap dust, mold, and pet dander. Opt for area rugs, which can be easily removed for cleaning.

Bring It All Up to Code

Any work done on an addition or on areas of a house that are being remodeled must meet current code regulations adopted by local officials. Although you're not required to bring your entire house up to code when you add on, now is a good time to do it. Not only will you save money by getting both the new and the existing spaces done as a package, you'll also save the hassle of trying to schedule the various trades yourself at a later date.

Wiring systems

Home electronics play an even larger role in day-to-day family life than they did just a few years ago, and the gear and the systems that run them have become much more sophisticated and complex. Codes that regulate such things as the design of standard electrical outlets or plugs, the minimum amount of voltage for a whole-house system, and the proper types and installation methods for electrical cable have been revised substantially in recent years. If your house is more than ten years old, it's unlikely that its wiring still meets code.

Plumbing system

Whether your plumbing needs updating depends on what part of the country you live in and what materials were used in the existing system. If you live in a region where seismic activity influences code-making policies, your existing system probably doesn't meet the latest requirements for safeguarding water lines against twisting, shifting, and wracking. If tap water in your area has high concentrations of lime or calcium, your water lines may be clogged with deposits. In many older residential areas, the pipe used for sewer connections between house and street no longer meets code and must be replaced if the system is expanded. In all parts of the country, codes require a water-saving, low-flow flush design for new toilets.

Insulation

The energy crisis of the 1970s triggered a nationwide code revision regarding materials and installation methods for insulating walls, attics, floors, and foundations. In many locales, extra inches to get the

---

BUILDING CODE CHECKLIST

How would a city building inspector rate your home's code compliance? Do an informal rating yourself by pinpointing potential problem areas with this system-by-system checklist.

Wiring
- [ ] All outlets fit grounded plugs
- [ ] At least 220-volt house power
- [ ] All exposed cables encased in metal conduit
- [ ] GFCI outlets in bathrooms, kitchen, and laundry

Insulation
- [ ] Vapor barrier inside studs
- [ ] At least 10 inches in attic
- [ ] At least 8 inches between joists above crawlspace
- [ ] Double glazing on windows and patio doors

Plumbing
- [ ] Low-flow toilet(s)
- [ ] Properly vented water heater
- [ ] Proper overflow drains in all fixtures
- [ ] Septic tank properly sized for number of bathrooms

HVAC
- [ ] Ridge or gable vents in attic
- [ ] Continuous rafter vents in soffits
- [ ] AC unit resting on solid base
- [ ] No condensation on interior surfaces of windows
- [ ] Furnace and fireplace flues drawing properly
- [ ] Propane tank on solid base

Safety
- [ ] At least one smoke alarm on each floor
- [ ] Railings on all decks and landings higher than 2 feet
- [ ] No more than 4 inches between balusters
- [ ] Windows in basement living areas big enough for exits

Structural
- [ ] No rusted pipe columns or leaning piers
- [ ] No heaving, cracking, or crumbling on basement walls
- [ ] No sags or dips in roof planes
- [ ] No bowed or tilted masonry in chimney chases
- [ ] Floors don't bounce or wobble

R-value (measure of a material's insulating properties with higher numbers indicating better insulation) are now required in attics and walls. Some codes now also require insulation on basement and crawlspace walls and under basement floors. Also, locales where infiltration or moisture barriers had not been required, such as in the Sun Belt and on the West Coast, now make these measures mandatory.

Keep Within Budget

No matter how carefully you estimate the various expenditures for your project, you're bound to encounter unexpected costs along the way. How do you keep these extra expenses from wreaking havoc with your budget? By building in a financial cushion up front and by watching for ways to shave expenses as the work proceeds.

Built-in backup

When you set up the financing for your project, be sure to add a certain amount to the contractor's estimate to allow for cost overruns. Generally, adding 15 percent to the bottom line of the estimate is an adequate amount. If your project is quite elaborate or involves some special challenges, such as a difficult site or extensive remodeling of a very old existing structure, you may want to boost your built-in cushion to 20 or 25 percent.

Budget-friendly design

As mentioned in Chapter 4, "Shaping the Design," eliminating unnecessary corners reduces labor and materials costs because it takes more time and creates more wasted material to build corners than to build flat surfaces. This is especially true for finish work because wrapping trim around corners involves complicated joinery. Elaborate detailing is also labor-intensive—either in the carpentry, in the application of finish treatments, or both.

Simple forms and surfaces are cheaper, but they needn't be bland and boring. One way to add visual punch without throwing your budget out of kilter is a creative use of color. Bold splashes of overall color can eliminate the need for pricey finish work in

order to make a style statement. Faux painting, a clever manipulation of color and pattern, can create the illusion of expensive finish treatments such as marble, dressed stone, or wood veneers. Color used as an additive with certain finish materials, such as concrete or skim-coat plaster, can produce inexpensive surface treatments that have pricey-looking patina and texture.

A bold swath of color turned this otherwise plain, featureless wall into a dramatic accent and focal point. It also functions as furniture; it doubles as the headboard for the bed.

Cost-Conscious Buying

Smart shopping is another means of keeping the lid on your budget and building up a little extra cushion against unexpected expenses. You probably should rely on your builder to obtain many of the basic products or materials, such as framing lumber, drywall, concrete mix, and other rough construction items. For key finishes, features, or focal points, however, such as paneling, cabinets, fixtures, doors, windows, tile, and flooring, you may want to do your own shopping in order to get exactly the right style, quality, and price.

Snagging bargains is largely a matter of being in the right place at the right time, which means your strategic shopping must begin as soon as you have a general design concept, not when the subcontractor is ready to install. Watch for closeout sales on building products (especially ones with big

Lining the sitting area with windows eliminated the need for pricey millwork; natural light and a wraparound view become major elements of the decor. An area rug adds a dash of color.

Simple forms and inexpensive finishes add affordable style in this budget-minded kitchen scheme. The built-ins are stock cabinets, and the "granite" top on the island is laminate.

markdowns on odd lots or discontinued items) at local lumberyards and home centers, and scan the classified ads for new and slightly used building materials. If you have a way of hauling home large or bulky loads, and can find a place to store them till they're needed for the project, you can usually realize major savings on a wide variety of items. Buying ahead of time and storing on site is called stockpiling—a strategy that requires footwork and foresight but that promises thousands of dollars in savings.

While you're studying the classified ads, keep an eye out for salvage, also. Although most salvage items are several decades old—they've either been, or are about to be, ripped out of structures that are being torn down—they are better-quality goods that would be prohibitively expensive if purchased new. Most, of course, are no longer available, which adds to their value even more. You might, for example, have to fork over a couple hundred bucks for solid slate countertops from an old high school physics lab, but you'd pay that much per linear foot for newly quarried material. Salvage goods sometimes dictate slight changes in design in order to make old shapes or dimensions fit a modern scheme, but if you buy far enough in advance, such tweakings are usually not a problem.

Phased finery

One other way to keep your budget on track is to postpone certain big-ticket finishing touches till your family finances have weathered the initial brunt of the project. Again, planning ahead is key here. As you fine-tune the design, tag certain features that can be planned for now but added at a later date with minimal mess and disruption. One example might be a fireplace. Another might be an elaborate kitchen island, or maybe an array of custom home-office storage built-ins.

Old mantels and bathroom sinks—items commonly found in salvage yards—offer rich detailing and character at prices that won't send your budget into a tailspin.

Though costing as much as a brand new stock window, art-glass salvage units are still a bargain compared to high-style custom-order units that are made to mimic them.

Gallery of Projects

Consider the age of your home to create a seamless look between past and present.

We've all seen additions on homes that look "tacked-on," or out of place with the original structure. To avoid such a costly mistake, one of the fundamental goals of any home addition is to blend the past with the present for a "meant-to-be," seamless look. By using the original architectural style of the home as a guide, you can remodel with respect to the home's heritage.

This 80-year-old Tudor cottage in Minneapolis regained its charm after several "remuddlings" over the years.

After removing the stuck-on back porch and sunroom perched above it, a slightly larger two-story addition was created with a family room on the first floor and master suite above it. As a result of careful remodeling, the home's outdated floor plan was given an up-to-date, family-friendly layout for year-round use. Just as important, the home's original Tudor styling, stucco walls, and sweeping rooflines were used to define the addition's beautiful exterior.

This new two-story rear addition offers the charm of a fairy-tale Tudor cottage and repeats the swooping rooflines and stucco exterior of the home's front facade.

What was once an unsightly porch is now a sunny, spacious family room. The vaulted ceiling provides through-views of the lake from the kitchen, and the transom in sidewalls add spatial stretch and more light.

Seeing the Upside

Adding a new upper level to a one-story home may be the best way to gain space, enhance views, and create dramatic styling.

When Tracey Komata and her former husband purchased this San Diego home in 1994, it was a small, two-bedroom ranch with 1,000 square feet of living space. Originally built in 1957, the house was also below street level, with no views. As architect Mark Christopher recalled, "Basically, it was a one-story, postwar beach house," he said. "It looked very much like a double-wide trailer."

To add the space and features the owners desired, Christopher proposed building a Craftsman-style addition atop the house.

The new second level would not only provide much-needed room, the addition would also allow for 12-foot ceilings with exposed beams, large windows, a new dining deck, and treetop views of the nearby beach. However, because the existing structure could not support a second floor, Christopher designed the addition as a "table on four legs." The original house now sits between the "legs" while the "tabletop" above it supports the upper level. By incorporating Craftsman design elements throughout the new addition and remodeled areas, the home gained architectural charm that it previously lacked.

Built in 1957, this one-story San Diego home—constructed below street level—lacked space and architectural style. A second-level addition was constructed over the existing structure and a bridge now connects the walk to the entry that is midway between the two levels.

An upper-level addition was built above an existing one-story home. This dramatic split-foyer entry unites the two levels and leads up to the living, kitchen, and dining areas on the upper floor, and to the original spaces below.

Main level
1129 sq. ft.

DECK

OPEN

DINING
13x9

KITCHEN
13x9

R

DN

DN

LIVING
21x19

ENTRY

PORCH

GARAGE
20x19

Using a Craftsman cruciform design, the upper level addition has four distinct wings of varying sizes. A few steps up from the front entryway of the house is the living area on one side. The dining area and kitchen are on the other side. Just off of the dining area, French doors open onto a dining deck which provides additional living space and treetop views of a Pacific beach. The smallest wing is at the back of the addition and overlooks the old living area below, which is now an office. The existing kitchen on the lower level was converted into a laundry room. Two original bedrooms were transformed into a guest room and a den.

Throughout the addition and remodeled portion of the home, Craftsman accents add continuity and character. Clear-pane windows were selected to enhance views from the home, and transoms above the windows bring in an abundance of light. Architectural elements were also used to distinguish one space from another. For example, the kitchen is hidden from the view of arriving guests by a half-wall that doubles as the back side of kitchen cabinets.

By considering the "upside" and adding the second level to the home, the architect created a classic split-level interior and more than doubled the living space. Generous use of natural cherry in cabinets, beams, and

The rear view shows the home before and after the addition was constructed. In the after view, the windows of the living area are on the left side, and the new dining deck is on the right.

BEFORE

In the dining area, cherry cabinets offer functional storage and repeat the Craftsman look found in the kitchen. Gracious French doors add a spacious feel and open onto the dining deck.

flooring give the house warmth. And the split-foyer entry offers easy access to both floors. A few steps down is the older portion of the house, and a few steps up is the new addition. What was once a dull ranch is now an upscale 2,700-square-foot Craftsman showplace.

An elegant kitchen atmosphere was created with rich cherry cabinets and artistic light fixtures. Transoms topping the windows over the sink provide additional light.

Cottage Connections

While a smaller home may be overflowing with character, its tight quarters may cramp your lifestyle. To satisfy your need for space, consider bumping-out and making big gains with a small addition.

This 1940s seaside bungalow on the outskirts of Victoria, British Columbia, was short on space. After serving as a rental property for 20 years, it also had become severely outdated, and an unattractive addition was put on the back in the 1970s. The kitchen was dark and cramped with little counter space. Plus, it was necessary to walk through the kitchen to get to the bedroom.

Thanks to a sensitive restoration and addition, the bungalow now lives well in the 21st century. To straighten out the kinks in the floor plan, an old deck and hallway off of the kitchen were removed and replaced with a bumped-out sunroom that now links the kitchen and bedroom. And with the goal of making all changes seamless with the existing structure, windows, doors, and moldings were reused wherever possible. Custom pieces also were built to match. In the kitchen, simple white cabinets with flush doors and drawers were constructed for a vintage look. Beaded-board on the exposed cabinetry further enhanced the old-fashioned appearance.

Between the kitchen and sunroom, a wall was removed to make both spaces seem larger and to welcome natural light into the kitchen. A custom-built French door, along with tall windows topped by triple-pane transoms, bring vintage flavor to the sunroom. Glowing, honey-color fir floors—which are used throughout the house—add warmth to the space. And a large skylight allows even more sunlight to spill indoors. For additional coziness in the sunroom, a fireplace was constructed with antique tile accents—a design element also used in the kitchen. Now, depending on the season, the sunroom can be used for dining or simply curling up next to a crackling fire.

The rear view of the home shows the new sunroom addition. The stucco exterior helps the sunroom blend perfectly with the rest of the structure.

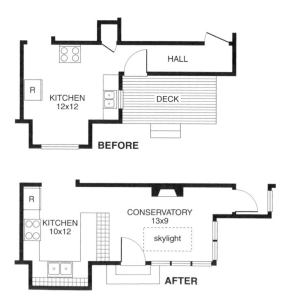

An old cramped kitchen was transformed into a modern, efficient space with extra countertops and a more compact work triangle. New cabinets were constructed for a 1930s appearance. Black laminate countertops feature cherry trim.

Although modest in size, the sunroom addition at the rear of the home adds substantial space and natural light to the small bungalow. Windows topped by triple-pane transoms look period-correct with the rest of the home.

Build a Multistory Addition

This view of the master suite from the backyard, *right*, shows a shallow barrel-vault ceiling that was made possible by cheating the height 2 inches on the sidewalls downstairs. Pairing transoms with doors and other glass sections, *left*, open the lower-level rooms to the outside.

Here's a common dilemma for many homeowners: You want to add square footage to your home, but there is little or no room to expand on the existing site. When space is at a premium, think "multistory addition."

That's what Tomas Tucker and Keija Kimuar did as owners of this century-old Victorian row house in San Francisco. To live comfortably with their child, the couple wanted to add a large dine-in kitchen, along with the privacy of a master suite and bath. With assistance from architect Michael Rex,

the couple's remodeling project began with the removal of an unsound 21×18-foot section from the rear of the house. In its place, a two-story, 28×18-foot addition was built with a kitchen and family room on the main level, and a lower-level master suite with access to the backyard and garden.

While the new addition has a somewhat contemporary look and feel, it echoes the Victorian character of the home for a harmonious blend of old and new. As a result of the addition, 979 square feet of space was gained in the home, but the overall change was even greater. According to Rex, the original, boxy interior of the home underwent a total transformation. "We replaced small tight places with wonderful, big open spaces; it feels as though they added more space than they did," said Rex.

A dramatic trussed-and-vaulted ceiling, French doors, and surrounding windows make the new family room/kitchen even more spacious.

Thinking Inside the Box

Every home addition presents a unique set of challenges. But due to a cumbersome floor plan and other obstacles, an abundance of creative thinking was required to remodel this Minnesota home on Lake Minnetonka.

First, owners Al and Cathy Annexstads wanted to convert the home's dark interior rooms to an open plan with multiple views of the lake. Second, the couple desired numerous amenities, including a vaulted great-room, two fireplaces, and an elaborate master suite. To top off the challenge, restrictive building codes prevented expansion beyond the original footprint of the home.

Residential designer Sid Levin created a number of ingenious solutions. In the great-room, Levin opened up the ceilings, eliminated walls and supported the roof with eye-catching architectural wood trusses. For natural light and better views, floor-to-ceiling glass-topped units with arched transoms were used. And a neutral color scheme was selected to further enhance the space. Natural tones appear in the cultured stone of the fireplace, maple floors, cabinetry, and granite countertops in the kitchen and bar area.

An existing staircase to the basement presented another remodeling challenge because it hindered the open floor plan. So Levin designed a cabinet and wall set up to hide the stairs while providing a bar and TV alcove.

To create the master suite, a 600-square-foot addition was built above the existing garage. Full-height windows, a curved cantilevered balcony, a gas fireplace, and a large-screen TV were installed. The spa-like master bath has marble accents throughout, a whirlpool tub, and walk-in shower. The room even boasts a full wet bar.

According to the owners, the home is now a perfect escape from the city. "It's so open and full of light," said Al. "What we have is an empty-nesters' paradise."

To remodel this Lake Minnetonka home, a master suite addition was built above the garage, ceilings in the great-room were raised and large arched windows were added for beautiful views.

A new sense of openness and a more functional floor plan was created by removing interior walls, adding arched windows and vaulted ceilings on the main living level. The natural—yet luxurious—maple floors, granite countertops, and leather furnishings enhance the spacious feeling.

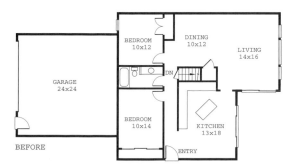

BEFORE

GARAGE
24x24

BEDROOM
10x12

DINING
10x12

LIVING
14x16

DN

BEDROOM
10x14

KITCHEN
13x18

ENTRY

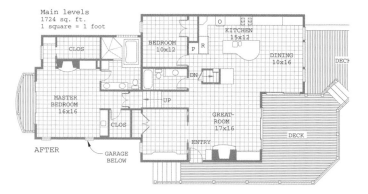

Main levels
1724 sq. ft.
1 square = 1 foot

AFTER

CLOS

BEDROOM
10x12

P R

KITCHEN
15x12

O

MASTER
BEDROOM
16x16

DN

DINING
10x16

DECK

CLOS

UP

GREAT-
ROOM
17x16

ENTRY

DECK

GARAGE
BELOW

Trading Places

If you want to build an addition on a vintage home—especially one in an historic district—it is best to prepare yourself for what could be a long-term project. But with ingenuity, patience, and plenty of persistence, nearly any dream is possible.

For inspiration, consider this 1890s shingled home, located in the Boulder, Colorado, Mapleton Hill historic district. When the owners Stacey Steers and David Brunel purchased the house, it needed work to accommodate their family. The home lacked informal living spaces and had no basement. Also, an addition had been placed on the rear of the house in the 1930s, but it was cramped and awkward. The owners turned to architect Steve Vosper for help.

To preserve the integrity of the main house while adding on and updating it, Vosper suggested tearing off the old addition and rebuilding over its footprint. The plans included adding a basement with a multispace addition over it that blended a modern kitchen, breakfast nook, and family room. The L-shape addition would also extend outward for a mudroom and patio.

The rear view of the family-room addition shows aluminum storm windows that were replaced with casement windows, a restored balcony above the porch, and stonework that was repointed and sandblasted.

MAKE A PLAN

Any home should be an attractive blend of materials, and the ones you select for the exterior of your home do not have to be the same throughout. A variety of materials, such as wood, brick, and stone, will work well together if carefully selected for texture and color.

The new kitchen features an artistic blend of vintage styling combined with modern conveniences, including a large island, professional range, and lots of counter space for dinner parties.

For a transition from the old to the new, the existing formal dining room was aligned with the breakfast nook and connected with a set of original pocket doors.

While the addition project was ultimately successful, sets of preliminary plans were rejected seven times by the neighborhood planning board before gaining its final approval.

Despite the setbacks and need to fine-tune the plans, the final result is breathtaking. The addition's family room, kitchen, and breakfast nook feel like individual rooms, but flow together gracefully for easy interaction. And the period detailing throughout the addition, such as wainscoting, coffered ceilings, wide trim, subway tile, and arch motifs, blend beautifully with

The fireplace serves as a focal point in the new family room. While the room is open to the breakfast nook, high wainscoting and French doors leading to a stone patio provide separation between the rooms.

the original turn-of-the-twentieth-century architecture. Adding even more functional space, the new basement houses a wine cellar, guest room, TV room, and laundry room.

"We use the house as it was originally intended," said owner Stacey Steers. "Formal spaces at the front; casual spaces in the back."

147

The sunroom and kitchen gives the family sweeping views from the upper level. All-white furnishings, open rafters, and ample windows add grace and elegance to simple sophistication in this sunny sitting room overlooking a meandering stream and acres of lush green woods.

Sunny Escapes

Situated at the top of a steep slope, overlooking four acres of lush green woods and a peaceful stream, this Detroit home simply ignored the beauty of the outdoors by providing only two window's worth of view. Built in the 1950s, this ranch offered nary a deck or patio for entertaining or grilling. The solution for the Bakken family came in the form of a multilevel cedar deck that not only embraces the family home, but graciously welcomes the outdoors in. Complete with hefty columns and posts, sturdy balusters, and wide overhangs, the new addition not only sizes up well with the existing home, but complements the heavily wooded setting it's embedded in.

On the lower level, a deck designed for enjoying the afternoon sun adjoins a screen porch—a wonderful retreat for the family in

This cedar deck is seasoned with stature—strapping columns and posts, sturdy balusters, and wide overhangs—making this a favorite summertime gathering place. Weathering all seasons, it provides a variety of activity zones for every member of the family.

the evenings during the mosquito-laden summers in Michigan. A landing midway between the upper and lower levels offers enough room for grilling and the option of serving family meals on either level. The upper level reveals the real reason this family took on the arduous task of this sunny addition—a year-round 15×19-foot sitting room flanked with windows and an incredible view. Originally slated for a second screen porch, once under construction the Bakkens decided the new room was

ideal for a "don't-bug-me" room complete with casual, easy-care finishes and simple decor. The no-TV rule reigns in this room where family members enjoy their quiet time and a small respite from busy lives.

Light-color, washable slipcovers for the furniture make it easy to keep this room neat and tidy even with five children scampering about. The rough-sawn paneling on the ceiling gives a comfortable feel to the room, and the vinyl-clad windows make this a wonderful carefree and maintenance-free addition.

This multilevel deck is the perfect solution for a steep hillside location. An ample deck and all-weather sunroom on the upper level, a larger deck and seasonal screen porch on the lower level, and a sitting area on a landing in between lets the family enjoy every aspect of their environment.

Growing Up **Gracefully**

Many homeowners take on very large remodeling projects so they can stay in their family home for one of two reasons: to remain in a particular area, or because they live on an exceptional piece of property.

The latter is the case for professional photographers Joan and Carl VanderSchuit of La Jolla, California, and their three young daughters. Their 1950s ranch collected the ocean breezes but lacked the coveted view they longed for. Standing on the main floor of their ranch, they caught mere glimpses of the Pacific Ocean. However, from the rooftop, the panoramic view was utterly breathtaking.

This prime piece of property had potential and would be a great return on any home remodel investment. Initially the home lacked a family room and dining room. The family hadn't used a snug breakfast nook for meals. Then they enlisted the help of a sunroom company to enclose their

covered back porch with clear panels to serve a dual purpose: family and dining area. Although the space was used, it remained inconvenient for serving family meals. The kitchen remained off in a corner, isolated from the rest of the main living areas. Meals had to be carried outdoors from the kitchen across the deck, or, on rainy days, carried through a bedroom to the sunroom.

Dissatisfied with the final outcome, the VanderSchuits finally moved forward with their remodeling plans. Enlisting the help of Ione Stiegler, an architect whose work Joan had often admired, as well as pho-

Prior to the remodel, the kitchen was isolated from the rest of the main living areas. After construction, the kitchen opens up to the dining room. A convenient door leading to a large back porch allows for ideal entertaining and easy access to family meals outdoors or in.

Large windows were added to the dining room plan during construction, opening up a stunning view of the backyard pool from the dining table as well as from the center island in the kitchen.

tographed, the exciting plans for this incredible transformation finally came to fruition after living in the home for more than 10 years. Stiegler concentrated all the efforts of the remodel in one area—ultimately cutting costs without sacrificing aesthetics. One-third of the house was torn off and a two-story addition erected in its place.

On the ground level, they created a new foyer, a great-room, a laundry, two powder rooms, and a double-car garage. On the second level, they added four bedrooms and two baths, increasing their square footage from 1,500 to an abundant 3,500.

Dual pedestal sinks stand at attention in the master bath, surrounded by storage units and recessed medicine cabinets. In the distance, a doorway leads to a private toilet and walk-in shower, allowing for privacy any time of day.

Not only did they add living space to their home, they also gained a nicer traffic flow, well-suited to the family's needs and lifestyle.

Adding a second story doesn't come easy. Several things have to be considered and kept in mind. Building codes have to be met and zoning checked to see if there are height restrictions. Structurally, the main level of the home has to be checked to see if it can withstand the added weight of another level.

Exterior changes, location of stairs,

mechanical and electrical system placement, disturbance of neighbors, and finally, disruption of your own life all have to be taken into consideration. In the case of this addition, the home had to be retrofitted to meet seismic requirements in earthquake-prone California. Removing a portion of the house and rebuilding would allow the homeowners to do just that without astronomical costs. The new space aesthetically works well with the original structure to maintain the small-house character and the cottage charm.

The VanderSchuits enjoy the fruits of their labor every day with a breathtaking ocean view from both the master bedroom and master bath on the upper level. Vaulted ceilings and an arch in the gable add drama and depth to the master bedroom suite stretching along the back of the house.

At project's end, classic millwork and creative built-ins accessorize the new interior. A built-in storage bench rests at the base of the stairway, hiding kids' shoes while offering a functional place to sit and put them on.

153

Four-Season Cottage

The transformation of this simple ranch home is quite dramatic. The addition created a generous dining area, additional storage inside, a new kitchen, and a courtyard worthy of long relaxing chats in a gorgeous garden setting.

Bumping out into the backyard to add space is by far the simplest and most convenient option for adding space to any home. Careful consideration should be given to building codes and restrictions when adding on to any existing structure. When that addition is an all-season room, don't forget to factor in the cost for landscaping, insulating, installing insulated-glass windows, and heating and cooling.

Here, the homeowners took advantage of a surplus of backyard space and created a new breakfast-nook bump-out complete with casement windows that open fully and give the effect of a breezy porch. Having windows on all three sides of the new addition captures coveted daylight and opens up a whole new view of their fabulous new courtyard. Keeping furnishings simple underscores the beauty of the garden outside. This new breakfast nook added much-needed space and an opportunity to enjoy a beautiful backyard garden spot that was not easily accessible before.

The new breakfast nook sports banquette-style seating for six with

Opening the casement windows on all three sides of this new breakfast nook turns it into a screen porch that lets in plenty of cooling breezes and fresh air. Sunrooms such as this promise to bring the outdoors in, therefore energy-efficient windows and doors should be an important part of the planning process.

under-the-seat storage that is convenient for kitchen linens and rarely used serving dishes. Just a few steps away, the red brick patio graces the yard with comfy patio furniture and promises rest and relaxation.

Also undertaken in this custom renovation, an extra, unused bedroom is transformed into the main part of a new kitchen, practically doubling the square footage of the kitchen. The new kitchen dons a custom-stained floor design topped with four thick coats of polyurethane that makes this high-traffic area both durable and scuff-resistant.

Lofty Ideas

When a work-at-home couple purchased
their 1970s ranch with limited space for
their family craft studio, they set their
sights on the space up above in the form of a
second-story gabled loft addition. To fit in
with the neighborhood houses, the exterior
of the house didn't change with the addition
of a loft.

Instead, opening up a loft melds practical workspace with parental responsibility.

While giving the homeowners the ability to
work in an office setting, they can still
hear and see what's going on with
children below.

Here, practical wood flooring, a
laminate-top work table, and lots of shelves
and cabinets combine for a practical, yet
user-friendly, workspace. An adequate
cleanup center complete with sink and running water, keeps messes confined and tools
organized. Fixed and casement windows
along the north wall following the roof
pitch offer extensive natural light while

helping to minimize glare on the computer screen. The white walls reflect a sense of peace and cheerfulness, making this modern-looking loft a winner to go to work in.

Strategically placed track lighting can either direct light to the intended workspace or illuminate a piece of artwork or the entire room. A beveled wall and open bookshelves serve as a balcony overlooking the living space below, adding visual interest and storage space at the same time. A comfortable sitting area at one end allows visitors to sit back and relax while they enjoy the asymmetrical shapes in this workspace.

A cleanup area, including a center island, keeps messes confined and workspace tidy.

Following the pitch of the roof, casement and fixed windows shed natural lighting throughout the loft, illuminating the entire room and spilling over into the living quarters below.

Artful Addition

The grid of windows forms a pattern on the north wall, providing natural light during the day. The same-size square cubes with subtle halogen fixtures serve as display cases for works of art. Italian porcelain floor tiles are durable enough to handle spilled paint, abrasives, and solvents.

Planning an addition for empty nesters with interesting hobbies can be somewhat complex. For Christina and Russell Keune of Arlington, Virginia, it turned out to be just that: complex. They both enjoyed rambling around town in their prized Packard, a 1953 convertible they had completely restored. As they considered branching out and purchasing another one, the lack of garage space had them worried. About the same time, Christina's business—rosemaling, a Norwegian folk art dating back to the

1700s—began to flourish. What they needed was an addition to meet each of these needs.

While other empty nesters were flocking to smaller homes, condos, and townhouses, the Keunes were contemplating adding more room—refeathering their nest, it would seem. Architect Charles Matta looked at every option for the bewildered couple. Their final design put everything into proportion—a compact two-story addition on the side of the original

house would give them the three spaces they wanted. A new garage would be added to the existing structure at the basement level with an additional room for Christina's studio set on top of the garage. An additional deck opening to the back of the house wrapped up what would be the perfect package for this creative couple.

The original home's architecture could not be matched. Instead they chose to make the addition special by giving it a contemporary spin on a Colonial revival. Artful stacking of windows and display cases form a square pattern on the interior wall and offer interesting lighting on the exterior at night. Ideally, the windows are set on the northern side of the home, providing natural light for Christina's artistic endeavors, while strategically placed lights on the interior show off her stunning works of art. French doors open from the studio to the deck and make this space ideal for entertaining.

Transom windows over the French doors to the new deck invigorate Christina's creative senses, while sunshine and natural light flood into the studio—prompting her artistic endeavors. Multiple lighting options also are available for any type of daylight.

The Keunes opted for a discreet basement-level garage on the back of the house so that it would remain invisible from the street. The craft studio's sloped roof, together with the tall ceiling, works well with the exterior design of the two-story Colonial home, while on the inside it creates a feeling of openness.

Index